THE INSIDER'S GUIDE TO SECURITIES LAWS

Navigating the Intricacies of Public and Private Offerings

Josh Luberisse

CEO OF

OTHER PEOPLE'S CAPITAL, LLC

The Insider's Guide to Securities Law: Navigating the Intricacies of Public and Private Offerings

Josh Luberisse

Published by Fortis Novum Mundum, 2023.

THE INSIDER'S GUIDE TO SECURITIES LAW: NAVIGATING THE INTRICACIES OF PUBLIC AND PRIVATE OFFERINGS

First edition. May 11, 2023.

ISBN: 979-8223650713

Written by Josh Luberisse.

The Insider's Guide to Securities Law: Navigating the Intricacies of Public and Private Offerings

By
Josh Luberisse

Table of Contents

DISCLAIMER:

Any content provided herein should not be relied upon as advice or construed as providing recommendations of any kind. It is your responsibility to confirm and decide which trades to make.

Trade only with risk capital; that is, trade with money that, if lost, will not adversely impact your lifestyle and your ability to meet your financial obligations.

Past results are no indication of future performance.

In no event should the content of this correspondence be construed as an express or implied promise or guarantee.

Trading carries a high level of risk, and may not be suitable for all investors. Before deciding to invest you should carefully consider your investment objectives, level of experience, and risk appetite. The possibility exists that you could sustain a loss of some or all of your initial investment and therefore you should not invest money that you cannot afford to lose. Futures, stocks and options trading involves substantial risk of loss and is not suitable for every investor. The valuation of futures, stocks and options may fluctuate, and, as a result, clients may lose more than their original investment.

The impact of seasonal and geopolitical events is already factored into market prices. The highly leveraged nature of futures trading means that small market movements will have a great impact on your trading account and this can work against you, leading to large losses or can work for you, leading to large gains.

The author of this book is not responsible for any losses incurred as a result of using any of our trading strategies.

Loss-limiting strategies such as stop loss orders may not be effective because market conditions or technological issues may make it impossible to execute such orders. Likewise, strategies using combinations of options and/or futures positions such as "spread" or "straddle" trades may be just as risky as simple long and short positions.

Information provided in this correspondence is intended solely for informational purposes and is obtained from sources believed to be reliable. Information is in no way guaranteed.

No guarantee of any kind is implied or possible where projections of future conditions are attempted.

None of the content published constitutes a recommendation that any particular security, portfolio of securities, transaction or investment strategy is suitable for any specific person. None of the information providers or their affiliates will advise you personally concerning the nature, potential, value or suitability of any particular security, portfolio of securities, transaction, investment strategy or other matter.

By reading this book, the reader agrees that under no circumstances is the author responsible for any losses, direct or indirect, which are incurred as a result of the use of the information contained within this manuscript, including but not limited to errors, omissions, or inaccuracies.

Preface

The world of private equity and venture capital is at once exciting and complex, offering the potential for significant financial returns but also demanding a deep understanding of legal and regulatory complexities. In the dynamic landscape of today's global economy, navigating this world requires not just financial acumen, but also a solid grasp of the many rules and regulations that govern it.

"The Insider's Guide to Securities Law: Navigating the Intricacies of Public and Private Offerings" is designed to serve as a comprehensive guide for those looking to understand the intricacies of the private equity and venture capital space, whether they are legal practitioners, investment professionals, or aspiring entrepreneurs. This book provides a deep dive into the various aspects of fund formation, regulatory considerations, deal structuring, and exit strategies.

Throughout the book, we take an in-depth look at the legal and regulatory considerations that underpin every stage of a private equity or venture capital transaction. We begin with an overview of the world of private equity and venture capital, including a discussion of the various players and structures in this space. We then delve into the nuts and bolts of fund formation, from selecting the right legal entity to understanding the roles of limited partners and general partners.

We also delve into the crucial area of tax considerations, discussing the ways in which private equity and venture capital funds are taxed, and exploring strategies for effective tax structuring. The book then turns to a discussion of the key US regulatory authorities that oversee this space, including the Securities and Exchange Commission (SEC), the Financial Industry Regulatory Authority (FINRA), and the Commodity Futures Trading Commission (CFTC).

In subsequent chapters, we explore the intricacies of the regulatory landscape, discussing compliance requirements, fiduciary duty, conflicts of interest, and the implications of the JOBS Act and other laws. We also delve into the important areas of anti-money laundering and know your customer compliance.

But understanding the law and regulations is just the beginning. The book also provides practical insights into the process of sourcing and closing deals, conducting due diligence, and managing and exiting investments. Each of these areas is explored in depth, with a focus on providing practical insights and actionable strategies.

As we navigate these complexities, we've included a glossary of key terms to help readers familiarize themselves with the terminology used in the industry.

In writing this book, I have strived to make the complex world of private equity and venture capital law accessible to a wide range of readers. Whether you are a seasoned professional looking to deepen your understanding, or a newcomer seeking to understand the landscape, I hope that this book serves as a valuable guide. The world of private equity and venture capital is filled with opportunities, and I hope that this book helps you navigate it with confidence and insight.

Enjoy the journey.

Part I: Introduction to Private Equity and Venture Capital

Chapter 1: The World of Private Equity and Venture Capital

Private equity (PE) and venture capital (VC) are two distinct yet closely related segments of the financial industry that involve the provision of capital to businesses in exchange for equity ownership. Both PE and VC firms play a critical role in the growth and development of companies by providing not only capital but also strategic guidance and operational support. While private equity typically focuses on the acquisition and management of mature companies, venture capital targets high-growth startups and early-stage businesses. This chapter will explore the world of private equity and venture capital, highlighting their similarities and differences, investment strategies, and regulatory landscape.

1.1. Private Equity Overview

Private equity refers to an alternative investment class where investors acquire ownership stakes in private companies or engage in buyouts of public companies with the goal of taking them private. Private equity firms pool capital from institutional investors, such as pension funds and endowments, as well as high-net-worth individuals. The primary aim of private equity investments is to generate long-term capital appreciation by improving the operational efficiency, growth prospects, and overall value of portfolio companies.

Investment Strategies and Stages

Private equity firms employ various investment strategies, depending on their focus and expertise. Some of the most common strategies include:

- Leveraged buyouts (LBOs): The acquisition of a controlling interest in a company using a significant amount of borrowed capital, with the acquired company's assets and cash flows serving as collateral. The goal is to improve the target company's operations, financial performance, and ultimately sell it at a higher valuation.

- Growth capital: Investments in mature companies with a proven business model and a strong potential for growth, often to finance expansion, acquisitions, or product development.
- Distressed investments: The acquisition of debt or equity in financially troubled companies, with the aim of restructuring their balance sheets, improving operations, and eventually selling the restructured company or its assets at a profit.

1.2. Venture Capital Overview

Venture capital is a subset of private equity focused on providing early-stage funding to innovative startups and high-growth potential businesses. Venture capital firms invest in these companies in exchange for equity ownership, with the expectation that a successful exit, such as an initial public offering (IPO) or acquisition, will generate substantial returns. Venture capital investments carry a high level of risk, as many startups ultimately fail, but a few successful investments can yield significant rewards.

Investment Strategies and Stages

Venture capital investments typically occur in stages, reflecting the evolving needs and risks associated with a startup's growth and development. The most common stages include:

- Seed-stage: Investment in a startup's earliest phase, often used to develop a proof-of-concept, prototype, or initial product offering.

- Early-stage: Investment in a startup that has a working product or service and is beginning to generate revenues but may not yet be profitable.
- Expansion-stage: Investment in a startup with a proven business model and growing revenues, often to finance further growth, product development, or market expansion.
- Late-stage: Investment in a mature startup with significant revenues and profitability, typically as a precursor to an initial public offering (IPO) or another exit event.

1.3 Similarities and Differences between Private Equity and Venture Capital

While private equity and venture capital share some similarities, such as their focus on equity investments in private companies and their reliance on pooled investment funds, there are also important differences between the two segments.

Similarities between Private Equity and Venture Capital

- Both involve equity investments in private companies.
- Both rely on pooled investment funds raised from institutional investors and high-net-worth individuals.
- Both aim to achieve attractive returns for their investors by growing and eventually exiting their portfolio companies.

Differences between Private Equity and Venture Capital

- Target companies: Private equity firms typically invest in mature, established companies, whereas venture capital firms target high growth startups and early-stage businesses.

- Investment strategies: Private equity firms often focus on LBOs, growth capital, and distressed investments, while venture capital firms concentrate on seed-stage, early-stage, expansion-stage, and late-stage investments.
- Investment horizons: Private equity investments generally have longer holding periods, ranging from five to seven years, while venture capital investments may have shorter holding periods, typically between three and five years.
- Risk and return profiles: Venture capital investments tend to carry higher risks due to the uncertainty associated with startups and early-stage companies, but also have the potential for higher returns if a portfolio company becomes successful. Private equity investments are generally considered less risky due to their focus on mature, cash-generating companies, but their potential returns are usually lower compared to venture capital.

1.4 The Regulatory Landscape

Both private equity and venture capital are subject to a range of securities laws and regulations, which govern their fundraising, investment, and reporting activities. Some key regulatory aspects include:

Fundraising and Investor Accreditation

Private equity and venture capital funds typically raise capital from institutional investors and high-net-worth individuals, who are considered "accredited investors" under U.S. securities laws. These investors are deemed to have the financial sophistication and resources to evaluate and bear the risks associated with private equity and venture capital investments. The U.S. Securities and Exchange Commission

(SEC) has established specific criteria for accredited investor status, which include minimum income and net worth thresholds.

Securities Registration and Exemptions

Private equity and venture capital funds generally rely on exemptions from securities registration requirements under the U.S. Securities Act of 1933. The most commonly used exemption is Rule 506 of Regulation D, which allows for the private placement of securities to accredited investors without registration, subject to certain disclosure and filing requirements.

Investment Adviser Regulation

Private equity and venture capital firms are typically subject to regulation as investment advisers under the U.S. Investment Advisers Act of 1940. Investment advisers are required to register with the SEC or state securities regulators, depending on their assets under management, and are subject to various fiduciary, recordkeeping, and reporting obligations. The Dodd-Frank Wall Street Reform and Consumer Protection Act of 2010 introduced additional registration and reporting requirements for private equity and venture capital advisers, including the mandatory registration of larger advisers and the submission of periodic reports on their funds and portfolio companies.

Compliance and Enforcement

Private equity and venture capital firms are subject to oversight and enforcement by the SEC, which has the authority to investigate potential violations of securities laws and impose penalties, such as fines, disgorgements, and industry bans. Firms must also comply with anti-money laundering (AML) and anti-corruption regulations, such as the U.S. Bank Secrecy Act and the Foreign Corrupt Practices Act (FCPA), which impose due diligence, reporting, and recordkeeping requirements to prevent money laundering, terrorist financing, and corruption.

Private equity and venture capital are vital components of the financial ecosystem, providing much-needed capital and strategic support to businesses at various stages of development. Although they share some commonalities, their target companies, investment strategies, and risk-return profiles differ significantly. Both segments are subject to a complex regulatory landscape, which aims to protect investors, maintain market integrity, and ensure the overall stability of the financial system. Understanding the intricacies of private equity and venture capital is essential for legal practitioners, business professionals, and investors navigating this dynamic and high-stakes industry.

Part II: Fund Formation and Structuring

Chapter 2: Fund Formation Basics

2.1. Legal Entities and Structures

Private equity and venture capital funds are typically structured as limited partnerships or limited liability companies (LLCs) to facilitate efficient management, minimize taxation, and provide limited liability protection for investors. This section provides an overview of the key features of these legal entities and their suitability for fund formation.

Limited Partnerships

A limited partnership (LP) is a type of partnership consisting of one or more general partners (GPs) and one or more limited partners (LPs). The general partner(s) manage the partnership's operations and have unlimited liability for the partnership's debts and obligations. In contrast, limited partners have limited liability, meaning their liability is restricted to their capital contributions to the partnership. Limited partners do not participate in the day-to-day management of the partnership and may lose their limited liability status if they engage in management activities.

Limited partnerships are commonly used as the legal structure for private equity and venture capital funds due to their flexibility, pass-through tax treatment, and limited liability protection for investors. Under a pass-through tax structure, the partnership's income, gains, losses, deductions, and credits flow through to the partners, who report their respective shares of these items on their individual tax returns. This avoids double taxation, as the partnership itself is not subject to federal income tax.

Limited Liability Companies

A limited liability company (LLC) is a hybrid legal entity that combines features of partnerships and corporations. An LLC is owned by its members, who have limited liability protection similar to shareholders in a corporation. The management of an LLC can be either member-managed, where all members participate in the management and operation of the business, or manager-managed, where one or more designated managers are responsible for the day-to-day management of the business.

Like limited partnerships, LLCs are generally treated as pass-through entities for tax purposes. This means that income, gains, losses, deductions, and credits flow through to the members, who report their respective shares of these items on their individual tax returns.

LLCs can also be used as the legal structure for private equity and venture capital funds, especially when a more flexible management structure is desired or when certain tax or regulatory considerations make an LLC more advantageous than a limited partnership. However, limited partnerships remain the most common choice for fund formation due to their widespread use and familiarity in the investment community.

2.2. Limited Partners and General Partners

Limited Partners

Limited partners (LPs) are the passive investors in a private equity or venture capital fund, contributing capital but not participating in the fund's management. LPs typically include institutional investors, such as pension funds, endowments, foundations, and insurance companies, as well as high-net-worth individuals and family offices.

Limited partners have limited liability, meaning their liability for the fund's debts and obligations is limited to their capital contributions. This protection allows LPs to invest in high-risk, high-reward opportunities without exposing their personal assets to unlimited liability. In return for their capital contributions, LPs receive a share of the fund's profits, typically in the form of distributions and capital gains.

General Partners

General partners (GPs) are responsible for the management and operation of a private equity or venture capital fund, including sourcing and evaluating investment opportunities, executing transactions, monitoring portfolio companies, and managing exits. GPs are usually organized as a separate legal entity, such as a corporation or LLC, to provide limited liability protection for the individuals involved in the fund's management.

As the fund's manager, the general partner is entitled to a management fee, typically calculated as a percentage of the fund's committed capital or assets under management. This fee is intended to cover the operating expenses of the fund, such as salaries, office expenses, and other administrative costs. In addition to the management fee, GPs also receive a share of the fund's profits, known as carried interest or carry. Carried interest is typically structured as a percentage of the fund's profits, subject to a preferred return or hurdle rate that must be achieved before the GP can participate in the profits.

GPs have a fiduciary duty to act in the best interests of the LPs, meaning they must act with care, loyalty, and good faith in managing the fund's investments. GPs are also subject to unlimited liability for the fund's debts and obligations, although this risk is often mitigated by organizing the GP as a separate legal entity with limited liability protection.

2.3. Fund Terms and Agreements

When forming a private equity or venture capital fund, GPs and LPs negotiate a set of terms and agreements that govern the fund's structure, management, and operations. These terms are typically set forth in a limited partnership agreement (LPA) or a similar governing document, such as an LLC operating agreement. Key terms and agreements in the LPA or governing document include the following:

Fund Size and Capital Commitments

The fund's size, or the total amount of capital to be raised from LPs, is a critical term in the LPA. The fund's size determines the scale and scope of its investment activities, as well as the management fees and carried interest that the GP will receive. Capital commitments represent the legally binding obligations of LPs to contribute a specified amount of capital to the fund over a defined period, typically three to five years. Capital commitments are drawn down by the GP on an as-needed basis to make investments and cover fund expenses.

Investment Strategy and Restrictions

The LPA typically outlines the fund's investment strategy, including its target industries, geographies, and types of investments (e.g., buyouts, growth equity, venture capital). The LPA may also include investment restrictions, such as limits on the concentration of investments in a single company or industry, to ensure diversification and risk management.

Management Fee and Carried Interest

The LPA specifies the management fee and carried interest arrangements between the GP and LPs. As noted earlier, the management fee is typically calculated as a percentage of the fund's committed capital or assets under management and is intended to cover the operating expenses of the fund. Carried interest represents the GP's share of the fund's profits, typically structured as a percentage (e.g., 20%) of the fund's profits above a specified hurdle rate or preferred return (e.g., 8%).

Governance and Decision-Making

The LPA sets forth the governance and decision-making procedures for the fund, including the roles and responsibilities of the GP and LPs. For example, the LPA may establish an advisory board or a limited partner advisory committee (LPAC) composed of representatives from the LPs. The advisory board or LPAC may have certain rights and obligations, such as approving conflicts of interest, reviewing valuations, or providing input on investment decisions. However, ultimate decision-making authority typically remains with the GP.

Distributions and Exit

The LPA outlines the procedures for distributing the fund's profits and exiting investments. Distributions are generally made on a pro-rata basis, with the LPs receiving their share of the profits first, up to the preferred return or hurdle rate, and the GP receiving its carried interest on any remaining profits. The LPA may also include provisions governing the timing and method of exit, such as requiring the GP to seek a public listing or a sale of the portfolio company within a specified time frame.

Term, Extension, and Liquidation

The LPA specifies the term of the fund, which is the period during which the GP can make new investments. The term is typically 10 to 12 years, with an option for the GP to extend the term by one or more additional periods, subject to LP consent. After the expiration of the fund's term, the GP must wind down the fund's investments and distribute any remaining proceeds to the LPs. The LPA also sets forth the procedures for the liquidation and dissolution of the fund, including the allocation of any remaining assets and the settlement of the fund's liabilities.

Key Person Clauses and Succession Planning

Key person clauses are provisions in the LPA that protect LPs in the event that one or more of the fund's key executives, typically the senior partners or managing directors, become unable or unwilling to continue managing the fund. If a key person event occurs, the LPs may have the right to suspend or terminate the fund's investment period, reduce their capital commitments, or take other actions to protect their interests. The LPA may also include provisions for succession planning and the appointment of replacement key persons.

Clawback and Escrow

Clawback provisions are designed to ensure that the GP does not receive more than its agreed-upon share of the fund's profits over the life of the fund. If the GP has received excess carried interest due to early successful exits, and subsequent investments do not perform as well, the clawback provision may require the GP to return a portion of the excess carried interest to the LPs. To facilitate the clawback process, the LPA may also require the GP to place a portion of its carried interest in an escrow account until the fund's investments have been fully realized.

No-Fault Divorce

A no-fault divorce provision allows LPs to remove the GP or terminate the fund without cause, typically upon the approval of a supermajority (e.g., 75%) of the LPs' capital commitments. This provision is designed to protect LPs in situations where they have lost confidence in the

GP's ability to manage the fund effectively, even if there has been no breach of the LPA or other misconduct. However, no-fault divorce provisions are relatively rare in private equity and venture capital fund agreements, as they can create uncertainty and instability in the fund's management.

Chapter 3: Tax Considerations

3.1. Taxation of Private Equity and Venture Capital Funds

Private equity and venture capital funds are subject to numerous tax considerations, both for the fund itself and for its investors. Understanding the tax implications of various investment structures, transactions, and strategies is critical to the efficient operation of a fund and its overall success.

Pass-Through Taxation and Entity Selection

In the United States, private equity and venture capital funds are typically structured as limited partnerships (LPs) or limited liability companies (LLCs) taxed as partnerships. These entities are considered pass-through entities for tax purposes, meaning that the fund itself is generally not subject to federal income tax. Instead, the fund's income, gains, losses, deductions, and credits flow through to the partners or members, who report their respective shares of these tax items on their individual tax returns.

This pass-through taxation structure offers several advantages for private equity and venture capital funds, including:

1. Single layer of taxation: Because the fund itself is not subject to federal income tax, there is only one level of taxation at the partner or member level. This avoids the double taxation that occurs with corporations, where both the corporation and its shareholders are taxed on the same income.

1. Flexibility in allocating tax items: Partnership tax rules allow for considerable flexibility in allocating the fund's tax items among the partners or members, enabling the fund to

optimize its tax structure to meet the needs and preferences of its investors.

1. Ability to utilize losses: Pass-through entities can generally pass through their losses to their partners or members, who can use the losses to offset other income on their tax returns. This can be particularly valuable in the early stages of a fund's life, when it may generate losses from startup expenses or unsuccessful investments.

Taxation of Carried Interest

A key tax consideration for private equity and venture capital funds is the taxation of carried interest, which is the share of the fund's profits allocated to the general partner (GP) as compensation for managing the fund's investments. Carried interest is typically structured as a profits interest in the partnership, meaning that the GP is entitled to a share of the fund's future profits but does not have a claim on the fund's underlying assets.

The taxation of carried interest has been a controversial and politically charged issue in recent years, as some argue that it represents a tax loophole that allows fund managers to pay a lower rate of tax on their compensation. Under current tax law, carried interest is generally taxed at the long-term capital gains rate, which is lower than the ordinary income tax rate, provided that certain holding period requirements are met. This preferential tax treatment is based on the principle that carried interest represents a return on the GP's investment of its human capital in managing the fund's investments, rather than a return on financial capital.

However, recent tax reform efforts have proposed changes to the taxation of carried interest, such as increasing the holding period requirement or taxing carried interest as ordinary income. Fund managers and investors should closely monitor any legislative developments in this area, as they could have significant implications for the after-tax returns generated by private equity and venture capital funds.

3.2. Tax Structuring and Strategies

Given the complex and evolving nature of the tax rules applicable to private equity and venture capital funds, it is essential for fund managers and their tax advisors to develop and implement tax-efficient structures and strategies that minimize the fund's overall tax liability and maximize its after-tax returns. Some common tax structuring considerations and strategies for private equity and venture capital funds include:

1. Leveraged Buyouts and Debt Financing: In a leveraged buyout (LBO), a private equity fund acquires a controlling interest in a company using a combination of equity and debt financing. The use of debt financing can provide significant tax benefits for the fund, as the interest expense on the debt is generally deductible by the target company for tax purposes. This can help to reduce the target company's taxable income and increase the fund's after-tax return on investment. However, fund managers must carefully consider the applicable tax rules and limitations on interest deductibility, including the potential impact of any changes to tax laws or regulations.

1. Tax-Efficient Exit Strategies: When it comes time for a fund to exit an investment, the tax consequences of various exit strategies can have a significant impact on the fund's after-tax return. Common exit strategies include the sale of the investment, an initial public offering (IPO), or a merger or acquisition. Each of these strategies can have different tax

implications for the fund and its investors, depending on factors such as the nature of the investment, the holding period, and the specific tax attributes of the parties involved. To maximize the after-tax return on an exit, fund managers should work closely with their tax advisors to analyze and evaluate the tax consequences of various exit strategies and select the most tax-efficient option.

1. Utilizing Tax Losses: As previously mentioned, one of the benefits of the pass-through taxation structure of private equity and venture capital funds is the ability to utilize losses generated by the fund. Fund managers can strategically manage the timing and recognition of gains and losses to optimize the fund's overall tax position. For example, if the fund has generated significant losses from unsuccessful investments or startup expenses, the fund manager might choose to recognize gains on successful investments in the same tax year to offset the losses and minimize the fund's taxable income. Alternatively, if the fund has generated significant gains in a particular tax year, the fund manager might choose to dispose of underperforming investments to recognize losses and offset the gains, thereby reducing the fund's overall tax liability.

3.3. International Tax Implications

Private equity and venture capital funds often invest in companies and assets located in multiple jurisdictions, which can give rise to complex international tax issues and considerations. These can include the tax treatment of cross-border investments, the impact of tax treaties and withholding taxes, and the potential application of anti-deferral and anti-abuse rules, such as the controlled foreign corporation (CFC) rules and the base erosion and profit shifting (BEPS) project.

1. Cross-Border Investments: When a fund invests in a company or asset located in another jurisdiction, it must consider the tax implications of the investment in both the home country of the fund and the foreign jurisdiction. For example, the fund may be subject to tax on its income or gains from the investment in the foreign jurisdiction, and the foreign jurisdiction may impose withholding taxes on payments made to the fund, such as dividends or interest. To mitigate these potential tax liabilities, the fund may need to structure the investment through a foreign subsidiary or a holding company located in a tax-favored jurisdiction, which can provide tax benefits such as reduced withholding tax rates or the ability to defer taxation on foreign income.

1. Tax Treaties and Withholding Taxes: The United States has entered into numerous bilateral tax treaties with other countries, which can provide tax benefits and relief for cross-border investments made by private equity and venture capital funds. These benefits can include reduced withholding tax rates on dividends, interest, and royalties, as well as the elimination of double taxation on income or gains from the investment. Fund managers should consult with their tax advisors to determine the applicability and impact of tax treaties on their cross-border investments and to ensure that the fund is structured in a tax-efficient manner to take advantage of these treaty benefits.

1. Anti-Deferral and Anti-Abuse Rules: As global tax authorities have become increasingly concerned about the potential for multinational corporations and investment funds to engage in aggressive tax planning and profit shifting, they have implemented various anti-deferral and anti-abuse rules to combat these practices. Private equity and venture

capital funds should be aware of these rules and their potential impact on their international investments.

a) Controlled Foreign Corporation (CFC) Rules: The CFC rules are designed to prevent U.S. taxpayers from deferring taxation on certain types of income earned by their foreign subsidiaries. Under these rules, if a U.S. shareholder owns more than 50% of the vote or value of a foreign corporation, the U.S. shareholder may be required to include its pro rata share of the foreign corporation's "Subpart F" income in its taxable income, even if the income is not distributed to the U.S. shareholder. Private equity and venture capital funds that invest in foreign companies through foreign subsidiaries should consider the potential application of the CFC rules and structure their investments to minimize the impact of these rules on the fund and its investors.

b) Base Erosion and Profit Shifting (BEPS) Project: The BEPS project is a global initiative led by the Organization for Economic Cooperation and Development (OECD) and the G20 countries to address the issue of multinational corporations and investment funds shifting profits to low-tax jurisdictions to reduce their overall tax liability. The BEPS project has resulted in numerous recommendations for changes to international tax rules, including new transparency and reporting requirements, the implementation of anti-abuse rules such as the "principal purpose test" for tax treaty benefits, and the development of a multilateral instrument to modify existing tax treaties to implement BEPS-related measures. Private equity and venture capital funds with cross-border investments should closely monitor the ongoing developments related to the

BEPS project and their potential impact on the fund's international tax strategy and compliance obligations.

Tax considerations play a critical role in the structuring and operation of private equity and venture capital funds. Fund managers must navigate a complex web of domestic and international tax rules and regulations to ensure that their funds are structured in a tax-efficient manner that maximizes after-tax returns for investors. Fund managers can effectively manage their funds' tax risks and optimize their overall tax position by working closely with experienced tax advisors and staying abreast of the latest developments in tax laws and regulations.

Part III: Regulatory Framework and Compliance

Chapter 4: Key US Regulatory Authorities

4.1. Securities and Exchange Commission (SEC)

The Securities and Exchange Commission (SEC) is the primary federal regulatory authority responsible for overseeing and enforcing the federal securities laws in the United States. Established by the Securities Exchange Act of 1934, the SEC's mission is to protect investors, maintain fair, orderly, and efficient markets, and facilitate capital formation. The SEC is composed of five Commissioners, appointed by the President, with one Commissioner serving as the Chairman.

The SEC has broad regulatory authority over a wide range of participants in the securities industry, including issuers of securities, investment advisers, broker-dealers, mutual funds, and other financial intermediaries. The SEC is also responsible for the registration and oversight of nationally recognized securities exchanges, such as the New York Stock Exchange and NASDAQ.

Some of the key functions of the SEC include:

- Reviewing and approving the registration statements of companies seeking to issue securities to the public
- Overseeing the financial reporting and disclosure requirements for public companies
- Enforcing the federal securities laws, including investigating and prosecuting violations
- Adopting and amending rules and regulations governing the securities industry
- Providing interpretive guidance on the federal securities laws

4.2. Financial Industry Regulatory Authority (FINRA)

The Financial Industry Regulatory Authority (FINRA) is a self-regulatory organization (SRO) responsible for regulating broker-dealers and their registered representatives in the United States. FINRA was created in 2007 through the consolidation of the National Association of Securities Dealers (NASD) and the regulatory functions of the New York Stock Exchange. Although FINRA is a private, non-governmental organization, it operates under the oversight of the SEC and derives its regulatory authority from the federal securities laws.

FINRA's mission is to protect investors and ensure the integrity of the securities markets by enforcing high standards of professional conduct for its members. FINRA's regulatory responsibilities include:

- Registering and licensing broker-dealers and their registered representatives
- Conducting examinations of broker-dealer firms and their registered representatives to ensure compliance with federal securities laws and FINRA rules
- Enforcing the federal securities laws and FINRA rules, including investigating and prosecuting violations
- Providing investor education and resources to help investors make informed decisions

4.3. Commodity Futures Trading Commission (CFTC)

The Commodity Futures Trading Commission (CFTC) is the federal regulatory agency responsible for overseeing the futures, options, and swaps markets in the United States. Established by the Commodity Futures Trading Commission Act of 1974, the CFTC's mission is to foster open, transparent, competitive, and financially sound markets, to protect market users and their funds, and to prevent systemic risk.

The CFTC has jurisdiction over a wide range of participants in the derivatives markets, including futures commission merchants, swap dealers, commodity pool operators, and commodity trading advisors. The CFTC also has regulatory authority over designated contract markets, swap execution facilities, and derivatives clearing organizations.

Some of the key functions of the CFTC include:

- Registering and overseeing market participants in the derivatives industry
- Adopting and enforcing rules and regulations governing the derivatives markets
- Investigating and prosecuting violations of the Commodity Exchange Act and CFTC regulations
- Providing interpretive guidance on the Commodity Exchange Act and CFTC regulations

4.4. State Securities Regulators

In addition to the federal regulatory authorities, each state in the United States has its own securities regulator responsible for administering and enforcing state securities laws, commonly known as "Blue Sky" laws. State securities regulators typically have jurisdiction over the registration and oversight of broker-dealers, investment advisers, and securities offerings within their respective states.

While the specific regulatory responsibilities and powers of state securities regulators may vary from state to state, some of the key functions of state securities regulators generally include:

- Registering and licensing broker-dealers, investment advisers, and their representatives who conduct business within the state.

- Reviewing and approving the registration of securities offerings made within the state, including coordinating with federal regulators through the National Securities Markets Improvement Act (NSMIA).
- Enforcing state securities laws, including investigating and prosecuting violations
- Providing investor education and resources to help investors make informed decisions.

State securities regulators work closely with federal regulatory authorities, such as the SEC and FINRA, to ensure a coordinated and effective regulatory framework for the securities industry. In many cases, state regulators may bring enforcement actions in coordination with federal regulators or may refer matters to federal regulators for further investigation and enforcement.

It is important for participants in the securities industry, including private equity and venture capital firms, to be aware of and comply with the requirements of both federal and state securities regulators. This may involve registering with or obtaining licenses from both federal and state authorities, complying with ongoing reporting and disclosure requirements, and adhering to applicable rules and regulations governing their business practices. Failure to comply with these regulatory requirements can result in significant penalties, including fines, sanctions, and the potential loss of licenses or registrations.

The regulatory landscape for private equity and venture capital firms in the United States is complex and involves multiple federal and state regulatory authorities. These regulators play a critical role in maintaining the integrity of the securities markets and protecting investors. Understanding the roles and responsibilities of these regulators, as well as the specific requirements they impose on industry participants, is essential for firms seeking to navigate the intricacies of securities law and successfully conduct their business within the bounds of applicable regulations.

Chapter 5: Investment Advisers Act and the Advisers' Fiduciary Duty

5.1. Registration and Exemptions

In the United States, securities offerings are subject to registration and disclosure requirements under the Securities Act of 1933 (the "Securities Act") and the Securities Exchange Act of 1934 (the "Exchange Act"). The primary objective of these registration requirements is to provide investors with the information necessary to make informed investment decisions. However, certain securities offerings and transactions may be exempt from these registration requirements under specific exemptions provided by the federal securities laws. This section will provide an overview of the registration process, key exemptions, and their relevance to private equity and venture capital firms.

Registration Process

The registration process under the Securities Act typically involves the preparation and filing of a registration statement with the Securities and Exchange Commission (SEC). The registration statement must include detailed information about the issuer of the securities, the securities being offered, the terms of the offering, and any material risks associated with the investment. The issuer must also provide financial statements and other financial information, which may be subject to audit by an independent accounting firm. The registration statement is subject to review and comment by the SEC, and the issuer may be required to amend the registration statement to address any concerns or requests for additional information raised by the SEC.

Once the registration statement is declared effective by the SEC, the issuer may proceed with the offering and sale of the securities to the public. In addition to the registration statement, the issuer is required to provide a prospectus to potential investors, which is a summary of the key information contained in the registration statement. The issuer and its underwriters, if any, are subject to liability under the federal securities laws for any material misstatements or omissions in the registration statement or prospectus.

Key Exemptions

While the registration process is intended to protect investors by providing them with necessary information, it can be time-consuming and costly for issuers. Recognizing this, the federal securities laws provide for several exemptions from registration that may be available to private equity and venture capital firms, depending on the nature of their securities offerings and transactions. Some of the key exemptions include:

1. Regulation D Exemptions: Regulation D, promulgated under the Securities Act, provides a series of exemptions that allow issuers to raise capital through private placements without registration. The most commonly relied-upon exemptions under Regulation D are Rule 506(b) and Rule 506(c). Rule 506(b) allows issuers to raise an unlimited amount of capital from an unlimited number of accredited investors and up to 35 sophisticated non-accredited investors, provided that there is no general solicitation or advertising of the offering. Rule 506(c) permits general solicitation and advertising but requires that all investors be accredited, and that the issuer take reasonable steps to verify their accredited status.

1. Regulation A+ Exemption: Regulation A+ is an exemption that allows smaller issuers to raise capital through a "mini-

IPO" process, with more streamlined registration and disclosure requirements than a traditional IPO. Regulation A+ offerings are divided into two tiers: Tier 1 allows issuers to raise up to $20 million in a 12-month period, while Tier 2 permits issuers to raise up to $75 million in a 12-month period. Tier 2 offerings are subject to additional ongoing reporting requirements and must include audited financial statements.

1. Section 4(a)(2) Exemption: Section 4(a)(2) of the Securities Act exempts transactions by an issuer "not involving any public offering" from the registration requirements. This exemption is generally available for private placements to a limited number of sophisticated investors who have access to the same type of information that would be provided in a registration statement. Issuers relying on the Section 4(a)(2) exemption must ensure that the securities are sold without the use of general solicitation or advertising and that the purchasers do not intend to immediately resell the securities to the public.

1. Rule 144A Exemption: Rule 144A is a safe harbor exemption under the Securities Act that permits the resale of restricted securities to qualified institutional buyers (QIBs), such as banks, insurance companies, and investment funds, without registration. Rule 144A offerings are typically used by issuers to raise capital from large institutional investors in a private placement, while providing those investors with the ability to resell the securities to other QIBs in a secondary market.

1. Regulation S Exemption: Regulation S is an exemption that applies to offers and sales of securities made outside the United States. The exemption is based on the principle that

the U.S. securities laws should not apply to transactions that occur entirely outside the United States and do not involve U.S. investors. Regulation S provides a safe harbor for offshore offerings, subject to certain conditions, including a prohibition on "directed selling efforts" within the United States and a requirement that the securities be sold in an "offshore transaction."

Relevance to Private Equity and Venture Capital Firms

Private equity and venture capital firms frequently rely on exemptions from registration to raise capital for their funds and to facilitate investments in portfolio companies. The most common exemption used by these firms is Regulation D, which allows them to raise capital from accredited investors, such as high-net-worth individuals and institutional investors, without the time and expense associated with the registration process.

When private equity and venture capital firms invest in portfolio companies, they typically acquire securities, such as shares of common or preferred stock, convertible notes, or other equity-linked instruments, in private placement transactions. These transactions are often structured to rely on the Section 4(a)(2) exemption or the Regulation D exemptions, depending on the nature of the offering and the investors involved.

In some cases, private equity and venture capital firms may also participate in Rule 144A or Regulation S offerings, either as investors or as sellers of securities. For example, a private equity firm that acquires a controlling stake in a public company may seek to monetize a portion of its investment through a Rule 144A offering to institutional investors. Similarly, a venture capital firm that invests in a foreign portfolio company may rely on the Regulation S exemption to offer and sell its securities to investors located outside the United States.

Private equity and venture capital firms frequently engage in securities offerings and transactions that are subject to the registration and disclosure requirements of the federal securities laws. By understanding the key exemptions available under these laws, these firms can effectively navigate the complex regulatory landscape and efficiently raise capital and execute their investment strategies.

5.2. Compliance Requirements and Best Practices

Private equity and venture capital firms must comply with various legal requirements and follow best practices to ensure they meet their obligations under the federal securities laws. Compliance requirements and best practices can be divided into three main areas: investor relations, record-keeping and reporting, and ongoing compliance.

Investor Relations:

1. Offering Materials: Firms should provide clear, accurate, and complete offering materials to potential investors, including a private placement memorandum (PPM) that outlines the terms and conditions of the investment, the investment strategy, the risks involved, and any potential conflicts of interest. The PPM should be updated periodically to reflect material changes in the fund's operations or investment strategy.

1. Due Diligence: Firms should conduct thorough due diligence on potential investors to ensure they are accredited investors and have the financial capacity to meet their investment commitments. This may include verifying the investor's income, net worth, and investment experience, as

well as conducting background checks to identify any potential legal or regulatory issues.

1. Investor Communications: Firms should establish a clear and effective communication strategy with their investors, including regular updates on the fund's performance, investment activities, and any material changes in the fund's operations or investment strategy. This may involve periodic reports, conference calls, or investor meetings, as well as timely responses to investor inquiries.

Record-Keeping and Reporting:

1. Record Retention: Firms should maintain accurate and complete records of their investment activities, including documentation of the due diligence process, investor communications, and any material agreements or transactions. These records should be retained for a period of time sufficient to comply with any applicable legal or regulatory requirements and should be easily accessible for inspection by regulators or investors.

1. Financial Reporting: Firms should prepare regular financial statements for their funds, including balance sheets, income statements, and cash flow statements, in accordance with generally accepted accounting principles (GAAP) or another appropriate accounting standard. These financial statements should be audited by an independent accounting firm and provided to investors on a timely basis.

1. Regulatory Filings: Firms should ensure they make all required regulatory filings with the SEC and other relevant regulatory authorities, including Form D filings for

Regulation D offerings, Form ADV filings for investment advisers, and any other applicable forms or reports.

Ongoing Compliance:

1. Compliance Program: Firms should establish a comprehensive compliance program to ensure they meet their ongoing legal and regulatory obligations. This may include the appointment of a chief compliance officer (CCO) who is responsible for overseeing the firm's compliance efforts, developing and implementing written compliance policies and procedures, and conducting regular compliance training for employees.

1. Monitoring and Testing: Firms should regularly monitor and test their compliance program to identify potential weaknesses or areas of non-compliance. This may involve conducting internal audits, engaging external compliance consultants, or conducting periodic reviews of the firm's policies and procedures.

5.3. Fiduciary Duty and Conflicts of Interest

Private equity and venture capital firms, particularly those that are registered as investment advisers, have a fiduciary duty to act in the best interests of their investors. This duty requires firms to act with care, loyalty, and good faith when making investment decisions and managing their funds. To meet this duty, firms should be aware of potential conflicts of interest and take steps to address them.

1. Identifying Conflicts of Interest: Firms should regularly assess their operations and investment activities to identify potential conflicts of interest, such as preferential treatment

of certain investors, undisclosed fees or compensation arrangements, or conflicts arising from personal or business relationships.

1. Disclosing Conflicts of Interest: Firms should provide clear, accurate, and complete disclosures of any material conflicts of interest to their investors, both in the initial offering materials and in ongoing investor communications

1. Managing Conflicts of Interest: Firms should establish policies and procedures to manage and mitigate potential conflicts of interest. This may involve implementing information barriers or "Chinese walls" to prevent the sharing of sensitive information between different parts of the firm, establishing decision-making processes that are free from bias, or obtaining investor consent for certain transactions or arrangements.

1. Allocating Investment Opportunities: Firms should establish clear and equitable policies for allocating investment opportunities among their funds and other clients to ensure they fulfill their fiduciary duty and avoid potential conflicts of interest. This may involve setting objective criteria for allocation decisions, such as pro-rata allocations based on fund size or investor commitments and documenting these decisions to demonstrate their fairness and consistency.

1. Monitoring Conflicts of Interest: Firms should regularly monitor their management of conflicts of interest to ensure they continue to meet their fiduciary duty and act in the best interests of their investors. This may involve periodic reviews of the firm's policies and procedures, as well as ongoing oversight by the CCO and other senior management.

Private equity and venture capital firms should be aware of the various compliance requirements and best practices that apply to their operations and take steps to ensure they meet their legal and regulatory obligations. By doing so, they can protect the interests of their investors, maintain a strong reputation in the marketplace, and mitigate the risk of regulatory enforcement actions or litigation.

Chapter 6: Securities Laws and Regulations

6.1. Securities Act of 1933

The Securities Act of 1933, also known as the 1933 Act, is a federal law enacted in the United States to regulate the issuance and sale of securities. The primary purpose of the 1933 Act is to protect investors by requiring companies to disclose material information about their securities and financial condition. The Act was the first major piece of legislation established after the stock market crash of 1929 and is a cornerstone of U.S. securities regulation.

Objectives of the Securities Act of 1933

- Provide investors with accurate and reliable information about securities being offered for sale
- Prevent fraud and misrepresentation in the sale of securities
- Establish a transparent and fair marketplace for securities

Key Provisions of the Securities Act of 1933

- Registration of securities
- Prospectus requirement
- Exemptions from registration
- Anti-fraud provisions

Overview of Registration

Under the 1933 Act, companies offering securities for sale to the public are required to register the securities with the Securities and Exchange

Commission (SEC). The registration process involves the filing of a registration statement, which includes detailed information about the company, its management, the securities being offered, and the risks associated with the investment.

Some of the key information required in the registration statement includes:

- Company's business operations and properties
- Management team, their backgrounds, and compensation
- Description of the securities being offered
- Use of proceeds from the sale of securities
- Financial statements audited by an independent registered public accounting firm
- Risk factors associated with the investment

Prospectus Requirement

The prospectus is a document that provides investors with a summary of the information contained in the registration statement. The purpose of the prospectus is to give potential investors the necessary information to make informed investment decisions.

The prospectus typically includes the following information:

- Description of the company's business
- Management team and their backgrounds
- Securities being offered and their terms
- Use of proceeds from the sale of securities
- Risk factors associated with the investment
- Summary of the company's financial information

Exemptions from Registration

The 1933 Act provides certain exemptions from the registration requirements, allowing companies to issue and sell securities without registering them with the SEC. These exemptions are designed to reduce the regulatory burden for smaller companies and facilitate capital formation.

Some of the most common exemptions under the 1933 Act include:

- Regulation A: Provides an exemption for smaller securities offerings of up to $50 million in a 12-month period.
- Regulation D: Offers exemptions for private placements to accredited investors and a limited number of non-accredited investors, with varying offering limits depending on the specific rule (e.g., Rules 504, 505, and 506).
- Regulation S: Exempts securities offerings made outside of the United States to non-U.S. residents.

Anti-Fraud Provisions

The 1933 Act includes anti-fraud provisions designed to prevent fraudulent practices in the issuance and sale of securities. These provisions prohibit companies and individuals from making false or misleading statements or omitting material facts in the registration statement, prospectus, or other communications related to the securities offering.

Violations of the anti-fraud provisions under the 1933 Act can result in severe consequences, including civil and criminal penalties, injunctions, and disgorgement of profits. Civil penalties may include fines and the imposition of liability for damages incurred by investors, while criminal penalties can involve fines and imprisonment.

The Securities Act of 1933 plays a critical role in protecting investors and maintaining the integrity of the U.S. securities markets. By requiring the registration of securities, mandating the disclosure of material information through prospectuses, providing exemptions for certain types of offerings, and enforcing anti-fraud provisions, the 1933

Act helps to promote a transparent and fair marketplace for securities. Familiarity with the key provisions and requirements of the 1933 Act is essential for companies, financial professionals, and investors to ensure compliance with securities regulations and avoid potential legal consequences.

6.2. Securities Exchange Act of 1934

The Securities Exchange Act of 1934, also known as the 1934 Act or the Exchange Act, is a federal law enacted in the United States to govern the secondary trading of securities, including stocks, bonds, and other financial instruments. The 1934 Act builds upon the regulatory framework established by the Securities Act of 1933 and aims to protect investors and maintain the integrity of securities markets by regulating the activities of broker-dealers, exchanges, and other market participants.

Objectives of the Securities Exchange Act of 1934

- Regulate the secondary trading of securities.
- Promote fair and orderly markets.
- Prevent fraudulent and manipulative practices.
- Ensure the timely and accurate disclosure of financial information by public companies.

Key Provisions of the Securities Exchange Act of 1934

- Creation of the Securities and Exchange Commission (SEC)
- Registration and regulation of broker-dealers, exchanges, and other market participants
- Reporting requirements for public companies
- Regulation of proxy solicitation and tender offers
- Insider trading rules

- Market manipulation and other prohibited practices

Creation of the Securities and Exchange Commission (SEC)

The 1934 Act established the Securities and Exchange Commission (SEC) as the primary federal agency responsible for regulating the securities industry in the United States. The SEC's mission is to protect investors, maintain fair and efficient markets, and facilitate capital formation.

The SEC is responsible for:

- Administering and enforcing federal securities laws, including the 1933 Act and the 1934 Act
- Registering and regulating securities exchanges, broker-dealers, and other market participants
- Reviewing and approving new securities offerings
- Overseeing the financial reporting and disclosure of public companies
- Investigating and enforcing securities law violations
- Educating investors and promoting investor protection

Registration and Regulation of Broker-Dealers, Exchanges, and Other Market Participants

The 1934 Act requires broker-dealers, securities exchanges, and other market participants to register with the SEC and comply with its rules and regulations. The Act also grants the SEC the authority to establish rules and standards for the conduct of market participants to ensure fair and orderly markets and protect investors from fraudulent and manipulative practices.

In addition to direct SEC regulation, the 1934 Act also provides for self-regulation by securities industry participants through Self-Regulatory Organizations (SROs), such as the Financial Industry

Regulatory Authority (FINRA) and national securities exchanges like the New York Stock Exchange (NYSE) and Nasdaq. These SROs are responsible for creating and enforcing their own rules, subject to SEC oversight, to regulate the conduct of their members and maintain the integrity of the markets.

Reporting Requirements for Public Companies

The 1934 Act imposes periodic reporting requirements on public companies to ensure that investors have access to accurate and timely financial information. Companies subject to these requirements must file various reports with the SEC, including annual reports (Form 10-K), quarterly reports (Form 10-Q), and current reports (Form 8-K) to disclose material events.

These reports contain a wealth of financial and operational information about the company, including:

- Financial statements (balance sheet, income statement, statement of cash flows, and statement of stockholders' equity)
- Management's discussion and analysis (MD&A) of the company's financial condition and results of operations
- Information about the company's business segments, products, and services
- Risk factors affecting the company's operations and financial performance
- Information about the company's management team and corporate governance practices
- Executive compensation disclosures

Regulation of Proxy Solicitation and Tender Offers

The 1934 Act regulates proxy solicitation and tender offers to protect shareholders' rights and ensure that they receive adequate information to make informed decisions. Proxy solicitation refers to the process by which shareholders delegate their voting rights to a representative (proxy) to vote on their behalf at shareholder meetings. Tender offers involve the purchase of a significant portion of a company's outstanding shares, often as part of a takeover or merger attempt.

The SEC has established rules governing the disclosure and conduct of proxy solicitations and tender offers, including:

- Requirements for the content and delivery of proxy statements and tender offer materials
- Disclosure of the identity and interests of the soliciting party or tender offeror
- Prohibition of false or misleading statements in proxy solicitation and tender offer materials
- Requirements for the conduct of shareholder meetings and tender offers, including voting procedures and timeframes.

Insider Trading Rules

Insider trading refers to the buying or selling of a company's securities by individuals who possess material, non-public information about the company. The 1934 Act prohibits insider trading to maintain a level playing field for all investors and protect the integrity of securities markets.

Violations of insider trading rules can result in severe consequences, including civil and criminal penalties, injunctions, and disgorgement of profits. Civil penalties may include fines and the imposition of liability for damages incurred by investors, while criminal penalties can involve fines and imprisonment.

Market Manipulation and Other Prohibited Practices

Market manipulation refers to the use of deceptive or manipulative practices to influence the price or trading volume of a security. The 1934 Act prohibits market manipulation to maintain fair and orderly markets and protect investors from fraudulent practices.

Some examples of market manipulation and other prohibited practices under the 1934 Act include:

- Pump-and-dump schemes: Involves the artificial inflation of a security's price through false or misleading statements, followed by the sale of the security at the inflated price.
- Wash trades: Involves the simultaneous buying and selling of a security by the same trader to create the appearance of trading activity.
- Spoofing and layering: Involves placing and quickly canceling orders to manipulate the market price or trading volume of a security.

The Securities Exchange Act of 1934 is a cornerstone of U.S. securities regulation, governing the secondary trading of securities and the activities of market participants. By establishing the SEC, regulating broker-dealers, exchanges, and other market participants, imposing reporting requirements on public companies, and enforcing rules against insider trading, market manipulation, and other prohibited practices, the 1934 Act helps to promote transparency, fairness, and integrity in the securities markets. Understanding the key provisions and requirements of the 1934 Act is essential for financial professionals, market participants, and investors to ensure compliance with securities regulations and avoid potential legal consequences.

6.3. The Investment Company Act of 1940

The Investment Advisers Act of 1940, often referred to as the Advisers Act, is a U.S. federal law that defines the role and responsibilities of an investment adviser. The law establishes rules for investment advisers to protect the interests of investors and maintain the integrity of the investment advisory industry.

Objectives of the Investment Advisers Act of 1940

- Define the role and responsibilities of investment advisers
    - Regulate the activities and practices of investment advisers
    - Ensure transparency and fairness in the investment advisory industry

Key Provisions of the Investment Advisers Act of 1940

- Definition and registration of investment advisers
    - Fiduciary duties and ethical conduct
    - Disclosure requirements and prohibited practices

Definition of an Investment Adviser

Under the Advisers Act, an investment adviser is defined as any person or firm that:

- Provides advice, makes recommendations, issues reports, or furnishes analyses on securities, either directly or through publications.
- Is in the business of providing these services.
- Receives compensation for these services.

Registration of Investment Advisers

Investment advisers who manage assets of $110 million or more are generally required to register with the Securities and Exchange

Commission (SEC). Advisers managing less than $110 million may be required to register at the state level.

Fiduciary Duties of Investment Advisers

As fiduciaries, investment advisers have a legal obligation to act in the best interest of their clients. This includes:

- Duty of Loyalty: Advisers must put their clients' interests before their own and must disclose any potential conflicts of interest.
- Duty of Care: Advisers must provide advice that is in the best interest of the client, based on a thorough analysis and understanding of the client's financial situation and investment objectives.

Ethical Conduct

Investment advisers are expected to adhere to high standards of ethical conduct. This includes:

- Fair dealing with clients
- Avoidance of fraudulent and deceptive practices
- Compliance with all applicable laws and regulations

Disclosure Requirements

The Advisers Act requires investment advisers to provide full and fair disclosure of all material facts to their clients. This includes:

- The adviser's qualifications, services, and fees
- The risks associated with the adviser's investment strategies
- Any potential conflicts of interest

Prohibited Practices

The Advisers Act prohibits certain practices that could harm clients or undermine the integrity of the investment advisory industry. These include:

- Fraudulent and deceptive practices

- Insider trading
- Churning, or excessive trading in a client's account to generate commissions

Enforcement of the Advisers Act

The SEC is responsible for enforcing the Advisers Act. This includes conducting inspections and examinations of registered investment advisers, investigating potential violations, and taking enforcement action when necessary.

Penalties for Violations

Violations of the Advisers Act can result in serious penalties, including fines, disgorgement of ill-gotten gains, suspension or revocation of registration, and criminal charges.

The Investment Advisers Act of 1940 plays a crucial role in regulating the investment advisory industry, protecting investors, and maintaining the integrity of the financial markets. Understanding the requirements and prohibitions of the Advisers Act is essential for investment advisers, financial professionals, and investors.

6.4. The JOBS Act and Emerging Growth Companies

The Jumpstart Our Business Startups Act, or JOBS Act, was signed into law by President Barack Obama on April 5, 2012. The Act was designed to encourage the growth of small businesses and startups in the United States by easing certain regulatory requirements and providing greater access to capital. One of the key features of the JOBS Act is the creation of a new category of companies called "emerging growth companies" (EGCs), which are subject to less stringent regulatory and reporting requirements than larger companies. This section will provide an overview of the JOBS Act, its provisions relating to EGCs, and the implications for companies looking to take advantage of these new opportunities.

The JOBS Act was enacted in response to concerns that the regulatory environment in the United States had become too burdensome for small businesses and startups, making it difficult for them to raise capital and grow. The Act aimed to address this issue by reducing the regulatory requirements for certain companies, particularly those in the early stages of development, and by facilitating access to capital through new and expanded methods of fundraising.

The JOBS Act consists of several key provisions, including:

- Title I: Reopening American Capital Markets to Emerging Growth Companies
- Title II: Access to Capital for Job Creators
- Title III: Crowdfunding
- Title IV: Small Company Capital Formation
- Title V: Private Company Flexibility and Growth
- Title VI: Capital Expansion
- Title VII: Outreach on Changes to the Law

Emerging Growth Companies (EGCs)

Title I of the JOBS Act establishes the category of "emerging growth companies," which are defined as companies with total annual gross revenues of less than $1 billion during their most recent fiscal year. EGCs are subject to a more relaxed regulatory regime than larger companies, which is intended to reduce the costs and burdens associated with going public and to encourage more companies to access public capital markets.

Key provisions applicable to EGCs under the JOBS Act include:

- Reduced Financial Disclosure Requirements: EGCs are only required to provide two years of audited financial statements when registering for an initial public offering (IPO), as opposed to the three years required for larger companies. EGCs are also exempt from certain financial disclosure requirements, such as the requirement to provide selected financial data for each of the five fiscal years preceding the IPO.

- Streamlined Accounting and Auditing Standards: EGCs are exempt from certain accounting and auditing standards, such as the requirement to comply with new or revised financial accounting standards until those standards are applicable to private companies. EGCs are also exempt from the requirement to obtain an audit of their internal control over financial reporting under Section 404(b) of the Sarbanes-Oxley Act.

- Confidential Review of IPO Filings: EGCs can submit their IPO registration statements to the Securities and Exchange Commission (SEC) for confidential review, allowing them to resolve any issues with the SEC before publicly disclosing their intention to go public. This can help EGCs avoid negative publicity and market reactions if their IPO plans are delayed or abandoned.

- "Test-the-Waters" Communications: EGCs are permitted to engage in "test-the-waters" communications with certain institutional investors before filing their IPO registration statements, allowing them to gauge investor interest in their offering before committing to the IPO process.

The JOBS Act and the EGC provisions have had a significant impact on the landscape of capital raising and public offerings in the United States. Companies that qualify as EGCs can benefit from reduced regulatory requirements and costs, making it more attractive for them to go public and access public capital markets. This has led to an increase in the number of IPOs involving EGCs since the enactment of the JOBS Act.

For investors, the relaxed regulatory requirements for EGCs may present both opportunities and challenges. On one hand, the easier access to capital for EGCs can provide investors with more investment opportunities in early-stage companies with significant growth potential. On the other hand, the reduced disclosure requirements and streamlined accounting standards may make it more difficult for investors to evaluate the financial health and prospects of EGCs, potentially increasing the risks associated with investing in these companies.

The JOBS Act and its provisions relating to EGCs have not been without controversy. Critics argue that the reduced regulatory requirements for EGCs may compromise investor protection by limiting the information available to investors and by exempting EGCs from certain corporate governance requirements. They also contend that the relaxed standards may encourage fraudulent or risky behavior by EGCs, potentially undermining the stability and integrity of financial markets.

Despite these concerns, proponents of the JOBS Act maintain that the benefits of promoting capital formation and economic growth for small businesses and startups outweigh the potential risks associated with reduced regulatory oversight. They argue that the Act provides a much-needed boost to the entrepreneurial ecosystem in the United States, which had been hampered by a decline in IPO activity and access to capital for small businesses.

Since its enactment in 2012, the JOBS Act has had a significant impact on the capital-raising landscape in the United States, particularly for EGCs. The Act has been successful in encouraging more small businesses and startups to go public and access capital markets, which has been an important driver of economic growth and job creation.

As the regulatory environment continues to evolve, policymakers and regulators will need to carefully balance the goals of promoting capital formation and economic growth with the need to protect investors and maintain the stability and integrity of financial markets. This may involve ongoing monitoring of the effects of the JOBS Act and its provisions relating to EGCs, as well as potential adjustments to the regulatory framework as needed to address emerging risks and challenges.

Chapter 7: Anti-Money Laundering (AML) and Know Your Customer (KYC) Compliance

In the world of finance, the importance of complying with anti-money laundering (AML) and know your customer (KYC) regulations cannot be overstated. These regulatory frameworks are designed to combat money laundering, terrorism financing, and other illicit financial activities by requiring financial institutions and businesses to verify the identities of their customers and monitor their transactions. In this chapter, we will explore the key components of AML and KYC compliance, the role of regulatory authorities, and best practices for meeting these obligations.

Anti-money laundering (AML) regulations are aimed at preventing the use of financial systems for the purposes of laundering the proceeds of crime or financing terrorism. These regulations require financial institutions and businesses to implement systems and controls to detect and report suspicious activities.

Know your customer (KYC) regulations are an integral part of AML compliance efforts. KYC requirements mandate that financial institutions and businesses verify the identities of their customers and maintain accurate records of their transactions. The primary objective of KYC regulations is to prevent financial institutions and businesses from being used, intentionally or unintentionally, by criminal elements for money laundering activities.

Several regulatory authorities are responsible for overseeing AML and KYC compliance in the United States. Some of the most notable agencies include:

a. Financial Crimes Enforcement Network (FinCEN): As a bureau of the U.S. Department of the Treasury, FinCEN is responsible for collecting and analyzing information about financial transactions to combat money laundering, terrorism financing, and other financial crimes.

a. Office of the Comptroller of the Currency (OCC): The OCC supervises and regulates national banks and federal savings associations, ensuring that they comply with federal AML and KYC requirements.

a. Federal Reserve System (FRS): As the central bank of the United States, the FRS plays a crucial role in regulating and supervising financial institutions for AML and KYC compliance.

a. Securities and Exchange Commission (SEC): The SEC enforces AML and KYC regulations for broker-dealers, investment advisers, and other entities in the securities industry.

a. Financial Industry Regulatory Authority (FINRA): As a self-regulatory organization, FINRA oversees broker-dealers and enforces AML and KYC compliance in the securities industry.

A robust AML and KYC compliance program should include the following components:

a. Customer Identification Program (CIP): Financial institutions and businesses are required to implement a CIP to verify the identity of each customer, including collecting and maintaining records of identifying information, such as names, addresses, and identification numbers.

a. Customer Due Diligence (CDD): CDD involves conducting a risk assessment of customers based on their profile, the nature of their transactions, and their anticipated activity levels. Enhanced due diligence is required for high-risk customers, including politically exposed persons (PEPs) and customers from countries with weak AML regulations.

a. Transaction Monitoring: Financial institutions and businesses should have systems in place to monitor customer transactions for unusual or suspicious activity. This includes setting up thresholds for transaction amounts, identifying patterns of structuring or layering, and monitoring cross-border transactions.

a. Suspicious Activity Reporting (SAR): Financial institutions and businesses are required to report suspicious activities to the appropriate regulatory authorities, such as FinCEN, within specified timeframes.

a. Record Keeping and Retention: AML and KYC regulations mandate the maintenance of accurate records of customer information and transactions for a specified period, typically five to seven years.

To ensure effective AML and KYC compliance, financial institutions and businesses should consider implementing the following best practices:

a. Develop a Comprehensive Compliance Policy: A well-documented AML and KYC compliance policy should be in place, outlining the roles and responsibilities of employees, procedures for customer identification and due diligence, transaction monitoring, reporting, and recordkeeping.

a. Appoint a Compliance Officer: Designating a qualified individual as the AML and KYC compliance officer is essential. This person should have the necessary authority and resources to implement and enforce the compliance program effectively.

a. Provide Regular Training: All employees, especially those involved in customer-facing roles, should receive periodic training on AML and KYC regulations, as well as the company's compliance policies and procedures.

a. Conduct Internal and External Audits: Regular internal and external audits should be conducted to assess the effectiveness of the AML and KYC compliance program, identify areas for improvement, and ensure adherence to regulatory requirements.

a. Establish Clear Lines of Communication: Employees should be encouraged to report any suspicious activities or concerns to the compliance officer or other designated personnel. A confidential reporting mechanism, such as a hotline or anonymous reporting system, can help facilitate this communication.

a. Collaborate with Law Enforcement and Regulatory Authorities: Financial institutions and businesses should proactively cooperate with law enforcement and regulatory authorities in their efforts to combat money laundering and terrorism financing.

a. Update Compliance Policies and Procedures: AML and KYC regulations are continually evolving, so it is crucial to keep compliance policies and procedures up to date. Regularly reviewing and updating these policies will help ensure ongoing compliance with the latest regulatory requirements.

Complying with AML and KYC regulations is crucial for financial institutions and businesses to prevent their involvement in money laundering, terrorism financing, and other illicit financial activities. By implementing a robust compliance program and adopting best practices, organizations can not only meet their regulatory obligations but also contribute to the integrity and stability of the global financial system.

Part IV: Fund Operations and Portfolio Management

Chapter 8: Deal Sourcing and Due Diligence

8.1. Deal Flow and Networking

In the world of private equity and venture capital, deal flow and networking are integral to sourcing new investment opportunities and building successful portfolios. This chapter will delve into the importance of deal flow, the networking process, and best practices for fostering relationships with potential investment targets and industry partners.

Deal flow refers to the steady stream of potential investment opportunities that come to the attention of private equity and venture capital firms. A healthy deal flow is essential for these firms, as it allows them to evaluate various investment prospects and select the most promising ones that align with their investment strategy and risk tolerance.

The quality and quantity of deal flow can have a significant impact on the success of a private equity or venture capital firm. A robust deal flow enables firms to:

a. Access a larger pool of investment opportunities, increasing the chances of identifying high-potential targets.
b. Diversify their portfolio by investing in companies across various industries, stages of development, and geographies.
c. Stay informed about market trends and emerging technologies, enabling them to make informed investment decisions.

Networking as a Key Deal Sourcing Strategy

Effective networking is crucial for generating deal flow in the private equity and venture capital sectors. By building strong relationships with various stakeholders, firms can tap into a vast network of contacts and resources that can lead to potential investment opportunities. Some of the key sources of networking in the industry include:

a. Entrepreneurs and Startups: Building relationships with founders and entrepreneurs can help firms get early access to promising startups and investment opportunities. Attending industry events, conferences, and startup competitions can help firms connect with entrepreneurs and stay informed about new ventures.

a. Business Brokers and Investment Bankers: These intermediaries often have access to exclusive deal flow and can introduce firms to potential investment targets. Developing relationships with these professionals can lead to valuable referrals and deal sourcing opportunities.

a. Industry Experts and Advisors: Connecting with industry experts and advisors can provide firms with valuable insights into market trends, technologies, and potential investment opportunities. These experts can also act as advisors on specific deals or help in conducting due diligence on potential targets.

a. Portfolio Companies: Existing portfolio companies can be a valuable source of deal flow, as they may have insights into their industry and can refer potential investment opportunities to the firm. Additionally, successful exits from portfolio companies can attract new investment prospects.

a. Co-Investors and Limited Partners: Building relationships with co-investors and limited partners can lead to collaborative investment opportunities and shared deal flow.

Best Practices for Networking in Private Equity and Venture Capital

To maximize deal flow through networking, private equity and venture capital firms should consider the following best practices:

a. Develop a Targeted Networking Strategy: Firms should identify the key stakeholders and sources of deal flow in their industry and develop a targeted networking strategy to engage with these contacts.

a. Attend Industry Events and Conferences: Participating in industry events, conferences, and networking functions can help firms meet potential investment targets, business partners, and industry influencers.

a. Leverage Social Media and Online Platforms: Utilizing social media and online networking platforms, such as LinkedIn, can help firms expand their professional network, connect with potential investment targets, and stay informed about industry news and trends.

a. Foster Long-Term Relationships: Building long-term relationships with stakeholders can help firms generate a sustainable pipeline of deal flow. This involves maintaining regular contact, providing value, and supporting contacts even when there may not be an immediate investment opportunity.

a. Track and Measure Networking Efforts: Firms should track

their networking activities, including the number of meetings, introductions, and deals sourced through networking. This data can help firms refine their networking strategy and allocate resources more effectively.

By developing a robust networking strategy and actively engaging with various stakeholders in the industry, private equity and venture capital firms can enhance their deal flow and uncover valuable investment opportunities. This process requires ongoing effort and a commitment to building strong, long-lasting relationships with a diverse network of contacts.

Building a Strong Reputation and Brand

A strong reputation and brand can significantly contribute to a firm's deal flow by attracting potential investment targets, partners, and industry influencers. To build a strong reputation and brand in the private equity and venture capital industry, firms should consider the following strategies:

a. Demonstrate a Track Record of Success: A history of successful investments and exits can enhance a firm's credibility and attract new investment opportunities. Firms should highlight their track record, expertise, and accomplishments to demonstrate their value proposition to potential investment targets and partners.

a. Develop Thought Leadership: By sharing insights, expertise, and opinions on industry trends and topics, firms can establish themselves as thought leaders and attract attention from potential investment targets and partners. This can be done through blogs, articles, whitepapers, webinars, and speaking engagements at industry events.

a. Engage in Public Relations and Media Outreach: Actively engaging with the media and promoting firm news, deals, and insights can help build brand awareness and credibility in the industry. Firms should develop a proactive media outreach strategy, targeting relevant industry publications and journalists.

a. Participate in Industry Associations and Initiatives: Joining industry associations and participating in industry initiatives can help firms connect with peers, influencers, and potential investment targets, while also demonstrating their commitment to industry growth and development.

a. Foster a Strong Company Culture and Values: A strong company culture and set of values can help attract talented professionals and investment targets that align with the firm's mission and vision. Firms should clearly define their values, promote them internally and externally, and ensure that they are reflected in their actions and decisions.

Utilizing Technology for Deal Flow Management

Technology can play a significant role in managing and enhancing deal flow for private equity and venture capital firms. By leveraging technology, firms can streamline their deal sourcing and evaluation processes, track networking efforts, and maintain organized records of potential investment opportunities. Some technology solutions to consider include:

a. Customer Relationship Management (CRM) Systems: CRM systems can help firms manage and track their contacts, meetings, and communications with potential investment targets, partners, and other stakeholders. These systems can help firms maintain organized records of their networking efforts and ensure that no opportunities are overlooked.

a. Deal Flow Management Software: Specialized deal flow management software can help firms track potential investment opportunities, evaluate deals, and manage due diligence processes. This software can provide firms with a centralized platform for managing their deal pipeline and improving decision-making.

a. Data Analytics and Market Intelligence Tools: Data analytics and market intelligence tools can help firms analyze industry trends, identify potential investment opportunities, and evaluate the performance of potential targets. These tools can enable firms to make more informed investment decisions and uncover hidden opportunities.

a. Collaboration and Project Management Tools: Collaboration and project management tools can help firms streamline their internal processes, improve communication among team members, and manage due diligence activities more efficiently.

By leveraging technology and implementing best practices for networking and deal flow management, private equity and venture capital firms can unlock new investment opportunities, enhance their portfolios, and drive long-term success in the industry.

8.2. Legal and Financial Due Diligence

Legal and financial due diligence are essential components of the investment process in private equity and venture capital. These processes involve a thorough examination of the target company's legal and financial standing to identify potential risks, liabilities, and opportunities. Conducting comprehensive legal and financial due diligence can help investors make informed decisions and mitigate potential risks.

Legal Due Diligence

Legal due diligence involves a detailed review of the target company's legal structure, contracts, intellectual property, employment, and compliance with applicable laws and regulations. Key aspects of legal due diligence include:

1. Corporate Structure and Governance: Review the target company's corporate structure, articles of incorporation, bylaws, shareholder agreements, and other corporate governance documents to ensure they are in compliance with applicable laws and regulations. Identify any potential issues related to the company's ownership, control, and decision-making processes.

1. Contracts: Examine the target company's material contracts, including customer contracts, supplier agreements, leases, licenses, and partnership agreements. Assess the terms, conditions, and potential liabilities associated with these contracts, and identify any potential risks or opportunities.

1. Intellectual Property: Review the target company's intellectual property portfolio, including patents, trademarks, copyrights, and trade secrets. Assess the strength and validity of these assets, as well as any potential infringement or licensing issues.

1. Employment and Labor: Examine the target company's

employment practices, policies, and agreements, including employee contracts, benefit plans, and collective bargaining agreements. Identify any potential labor disputes, compliance issues, or other risks related to employment.

1. Regulatory Compliance: Assess the target company's compliance with applicable laws and regulations, such as securities laws, environmental regulations, and industry-specific regulations. Identify any potential violations, fines, or penalties that could impact the company's operations or financial performance.

Financial Due Diligence

Financial due diligence involves a comprehensive analysis of the target company's financial performance, position, and projections. Key aspects of financial due diligence include:

1. Financial Statements: Review the target company's historical financial statements, including income statements, balance sheets, and cash flow statements. Assess the company's financial performance, trends, and ratios to identify potential risks, opportunities, and areas for further investigation.

1. Projections and Forecasts: Analyze the target company's financial projections and forecasts, and assess their reasonableness based on historical performance, industry trends, and other relevant factors. Identify any potential discrepancies or unrealistic assumptions that could impact the company's future performance.

1. Working Capital and Liquidity: Evaluate the target company's working capital and liquidity position, including

its current assets, current liabilities, and cash flow management. Assess the company's ability to meet its short-term obligations and identify any potential liquidity risks.

1. Capital Structure and Debt: Review the target company's capital structure and debt obligations, including the terms, conditions, and covenants associated with its debt instruments. Assess the company's debt capacity and potential refinancing or restructuring opportunities.

1. Tax Matters: Examine the target company's tax filings, liabilities, and planning strategies. Identify any potential tax risks, exposures, or opportunities that could impact the company's financial performance and valuation.

8.3. Industry-Specific Due Diligence

In addition to legal and financial due diligence, private equity and venture capital investors should also conduct industry-specific due diligence to assess the target company's competitive position, growth prospects, and potential risks within its industry. Key aspects of industry-specific due diligence include:

1. Market Analysis: Assess the target company's market size, growth trends, and competitive landscape. Identify the key drivers of growth and potential risks within the industry, as well as the company's competitive advantages and vulnerabilities.

1. Customer and Supplier Analysis: Review the target company's customer base and supplier relationships, including their concentration, stability, and creditworthiness. Evaluate the company's reliance on key customers or

suppliers, as well as any potential risks or opportunities related to these relationships.

1. Product and Service Analysis: Examine the target company's products and services, including their features, benefits, and market positioning. Assess the company's product development pipeline, innovation capabilities, and potential risks related to product obsolescence or changing customer preferences.

1. Operational Analysis: Review the target company's operations, including its manufacturing, distribution, and sales processes. Assess the company's efficiency, capacity utilization, and potential cost savings or improvements that could be achieved through operational enhancements.

1. Regulatory and Legal Environment: Evaluate the target company's exposure to industry-specific regulations and legal requirements, such as product safety standards, environmental regulations, and licensing requirements. Identify any potential compliance risks, liabilities, or opportunities related to these industry-specific regulations.

Conducting thorough legal, financial, and industry-specific due diligence is critical for private equity and venture capital investors to make informed investment decisions and minimize potential risks. By carefully examining the target company's legal and financial standing, as well as its competitive position within its industry, investors can identify potential risks, opportunities, and value drivers that will ultimately impact the success of their investment.

Chapter 9: Transaction Structuring and Execution

9.1. Deal Terms and Negotiation

Deal terms and negotiation are crucial aspects of private equity and venture capital transactions. They involve a complex interplay of various factors that influence the overall structure, valuation, and risk allocation of a deal. Understanding the key components of deal terms and negotiations can help investors achieve their desired outcomes and optimize the value of their investments.

1. Valuation: Valuation is a fundamental aspect of deal terms and negotiations. It involves determining the appropriate value of a target company, taking into account factors such as its financial performance, growth prospects, competitive position, and industry dynamics. Various valuation methods, such as discounted cash flow analysis, multiples analysis, and precedent transactions analysis, can be used to arrive at a fair value. Negotiations around valuation often involve discussions on the appropriate valuation method, assumptions, and adjustments, as well as the inclusion of earnouts or other contingent payments tied to future performance.

1. Deal Structure: The structure of a deal refers to the way in which the transaction is organized, such as the type of investment (equity or debt), the nature of the securities issued (preferred or common stock), and the allocation of ownership and control rights among the investors and existing shareholders. Deal structure negotiations may include discussions on the appropriate mix of debt and equity

financing, the terms of any preferred stock (such as liquidation preferences, dividend rights, and conversion rights), and the rights and protections afforded to minority shareholders.

1. Governance and Control: Governance and control provisions address the management and oversight of the target company, as well as the rights and responsibilities of the various stakeholders. Key governance and control provisions in deal terms and negotiations may include board representation, voting rights, information rights, and protective provisions (such as approval rights over major decisions or transactions). Negotiations around governance and control often involve balancing the interests of investors seeking to protect their investment and influence company strategy with the interests of founders and management seeking to retain operational control and flexibility.

1. Exit Strategy: The exit strategy is a critical aspect of deal terms and negotiations, as it outlines the investors' plan for realizing their investment returns. Exit strategies may include an initial public offering (IPO), a trade sale, or a secondary buyout. Deal terms and negotiations around exit strategies may involve discussions on the timing and conditions of exit events, as well as any restrictions or rights of first refusal that may apply to the sale of shares.

1. Risk Allocation: Risk allocation refers to the way in which the various risks and uncertainties inherent in a transaction are distributed among the parties involved. In deal terms and negotiations, risk allocation may involve discussions on representations and warranties, indemnification provisions, and conditions precedent. The objective of these negotiations

is to ensure that each party bears an appropriate level of risk relative to its involvement in the transaction and its ability to mitigate or control the relevant risks.

Deal terms and negotiations in private equity and venture capital transactions can be complex and multifaceted, requiring a deep understanding of the key issues and trade-offs involved. By carefully considering the various aspects of valuation, deal structure, governance and control, exit strategy, and risk allocation, investors can achieve their desired investment outcomes and maximize the value of their deals.

9.2. Financing and Capital Structure

In private equity and venture capital transactions, financing and capital structure play a critical role in determining the overall success and risk profile of an investment. A well-designed capital structure can help to optimize the value of an investment, minimize the cost of capital, and provide the necessary financial resources to support the growth and development of the target company. In this section, we will discuss the key considerations and components of financing and capital structure in private equity and venture capital deals.

1. Types of Financing: There are several types of financing available to private equity and venture capital investors, each with its own unique characteristics, risks, and rewards. The most common types of financing include:

a. Equity Financing: Equity financing involves the issuance of new shares in the target company in exchange for capital from investors. Equity investors generally have ownership and control rights in the company, as well as the potential for capital appreciation and dividends. However, they also bear the risk of loss if the company underperforms.

a. Debt Financing: Debt financing involves the issuance of loans or other debt instruments by the target company to raise capital from investors. Debt investors generally have priority over equity investors in the event of a liquidation and receive interest payments on their investment. However, they do not have ownership or control rights in the company and have limited upside potential.

a. Convertible Securities: Convertible securities are hybrid instruments that combine features of both debt and equity financing. They can be converted into equity under certain conditions, such as the achievement of specific performance milestones or the occurrence of a predetermined event (e.g., an IPO). Convertible securities offer investors a combination of downside protection and upside potential, while also providing companies with the flexibility to manage their capital structure.

1. Capital Structure Optimization: In structuring a private equity or venture capital deal, it is important to consider the optimal mix of debt and equity financing, as well as the appropriate terms and conditions for each type of financing. Factors that can influence the optimal capital structure include the target company's cash flow and profitability, its growth prospects, its risk profile, and the availability and cost of different types of financing. The goal of capital structure optimization is to minimize the cost of capital while also providing sufficient financial resources and flexibility for the company to achieve its strategic objectives.

1. Financing Terms and Conditions: The terms and conditions

of financing in private equity and venture capital transactions can have a significant impact on the overall risk and return profile of an investment. Key terms and conditions to consider include:

a. Valuation and Pricing: The valuation of the target company and the pricing of the securities being issued are critical factors that can influence the potential return on investment for investors. Negotiating favorable valuation and pricing terms can help to maximize the value of an investment and minimize dilution for existing shareholders.

a. Dividend and Interest Rates: The dividend rate for equity securities and the interest rate for debt securities are important components of the cost of capital for the target company. Negotiating competitive dividend and interest rates can help to minimize the cost of capital and enhance the overall value of an investment.

a. Covenants and Protective Provisions: Covenants and protective provisions in financing agreements can help to manage risk and protect the interests of investors. These provisions may include financial covenants (e.g., maintaining certain financial ratios or levels of profitability), operational covenants (e.g., restrictions on acquisitions or capital expenditures), and protective provisions (e.g., approval rights over major decisions or transactions).

1. Syndication and Co-Investments: In some private equity and venture capital transactions, multiple investors may participate in a financing round through syndication or co-investments. Syndication involves the pooling of capital from multiple investors to provide financing for a single

transaction , while co-investments involve individual investors participating alongside a lead investor in a financing round. Syndication and co-investments can help to diversify risk, increase the amount of capital available for investment, and facilitate collaboration among investors with complementary skills and resources.

1. Exit Strategies and Capital Structure: The capital structure of a private equity or venture capital investment can also have implications for exit strategies and the realization of investment returns. A well-designed capital structure can help to facilitate exits through various methods, such as:

a. Initial Public Offerings (IPOs): In an IPO, a company issues new shares to the public and lists its securities on a stock exchange, providing liquidity for existing shareholders and raising additional capital for the company. The terms and conditions of a company's capital structure, including the conversion rights of convertible securities, can influence the attractiveness of an IPO and the potential return for investors.

a. Mergers and Acquisitions (M&A): M&A transactions involve the sale or merger of a company with another company, providing an exit opportunity for existing shareholders. The capital structure of a target company can influence the attractiveness of an M&A transaction and the potential return for investors, particularly in terms of the allocation of proceeds among different classes of securities and the treatment of outstanding debt.

a. Secondary Sales: Secondary sales involve the transfer of existing securities from one investor to another, providing liquidity for existing shareholders without raising new capital for the company. The capital structure of a company can influence the marketability of its securities in secondary sales, as well as the potential return for investors.

Financing and capital structure are critical components of private equity and venture capital transactions, with significant implications for the overall risk and return profile of an investment. By carefully considering the various types of financing, optimizing the capital structure, and negotiating favorable terms and conditions, investors can help to enhance the value of their investments and achieve their strategic objectives.

9.3. Closing and Post-Closing Considerations

Closing a private equity or venture capital transaction is a complex process that involves various steps, such as finalizing the transaction documents, obtaining necessary approvals and consents, and satisfying any conditions precedent. Once the transaction has been successfully closed, post-closing considerations come into play, which are crucial for managing the ongoing relationship between the investors and the portfolio company, as well as for monitoring and protecting the investment. In this section, we will discuss some key closing and post-closing considerations for private equity and venture capital transactions.

1. Finalizing Transaction Documents: Prior to closing, the parties to a private equity or venture capital transaction must finalize and execute the transaction documents, which typically include the investment agreement, shareholders' agreement, and any necessary amendments to the company's

organizational documents. These documents set forth the terms and conditions of the investment, as well as the rights and obligations of the various parties. It is essential to carefully review and negotiate these documents to ensure that they accurately reflect the parties' intentions and provide adequate protections for the investor's interests.

1. Obtaining Approvals and Consents: Depending on the nature of the transaction and the parties involved, various approvals and consents may be required before the transaction can be closed. These may include approvals from governmental or regulatory authorities, consents from third-party lenders or other stakeholders, and any necessary corporate approvals from the portfolio company or the investor. It is essential to identify and obtain any required approvals and consents in a timely manner to avoid potential delays or complications in closing the transaction.

1. Satisfying Conditions Precedent: Many private equity and venture capital transactions are subject to certain conditions precedent, which must be satisfied before the transaction can be closed. These conditions may include the completion of due diligence, obtaining necessary approvals and consents, or the occurrence of specific events or milestones. It is essential for the parties to carefully monitor the satisfaction of any conditions precedent and to take any necessary steps to ensure that these conditions are met in a timely manner.

1. Closing Mechanics: The closing process for a private equity or venture capital transaction typically involves the exchange of executed transaction documents, the payment of the purchase price, and the issuance of securities to the investor. The closing mechanics may vary depending on the nature of

the transaction, the parties involved, and the applicable laws and regulations. It is important for the parties to carefully coordinate the closing mechanics to ensure a smooth and efficient closing process.

1. Post-Closing Governance and Monitoring: Once a private equity or venture capital transaction has been closed, the investor's focus shifts to the ongoing governance and monitoring of the portfolio company. This may involve the appointment of investor representatives to the company's board of directors, the establishment of investor rights and protections, and the implementation of reporting and information rights. Effective governance and monitoring can help to ensure that the portfolio company's management team remains accountable to its shareholders and that the investor's interests are protected throughout the life of the investment.

1. Exit Strategy and Planning: From the outset of a private equity or venture capital investment, the investor should have a clear exit strategy in mind, as the ultimate goal is to realize a return on the investment. Exit strategies may include an initial public offering (IPO), a merger or acquisition, or a secondary sale of the investor's securities. It is essential for the investor to continuously monitor the performance of the portfolio company and the market conditions, and to be proactive in planning and executing the most appropriate exit strategy.

1. Ongoing Legal and Regulatory Compliance: Following the closing of a private equity or venture capital transaction, the portfolio company must continue to comply with applicable laws and regulations. This may include securities laws,

corporate governance requirements, tax laws, and industry-specific regulations. The investor should work closely with the portfolio company to ensure ongoing compliance and to address any potential issues or concerns as they arise. Failure to maintain compliance can lead to significant penalties, reputational damage, and potential loss of investor value.

1. Portfolio Company Support and Value Creation: In addition to monitoring the performance and governance of the portfolio company, the investor may also play an active role in supporting the company's growth and value creation. This can include providing strategic guidance, operational expertise, access to industry networks, and additional financing as needed. By actively supporting the portfolio company, the investor can help to drive growth, improve operational efficiencies, and ultimately enhance the value of the investment.

1. Risk Management: Throughout the life of a private equity or venture capital investment, the investor should be vigilant in identifying and managing potential risks. This may involve monitoring the portfolio company's financial performance, industry trends, competitive landscape, and regulatory environment. It may also include engaging in proactive risk mitigation strategies, such as diversifying the investment portfolio, implementing robust governance structures, and obtaining insurance coverage where appropriate. Effective risk management can help to protect the investor's interests and enhance the likelihood of a successful investment outcome.

1. Investor Reporting and Communication: Maintaining open and transparent communication with the investor is essential

for building trust and fostering a strong working relationship. The portfolio company should provide regular financial and operational updates, as well as any other information that may be relevant to the investor's interests. The investor, in turn, should provide feedback and guidance to the portfolio company, and should be responsive to any requests for information or support. Effective communication can help to align the interests of the investor and the portfolio company and promote a collaborative approach to value creation.

By understanding and addressing these closing and post-closing considerations, investors and portfolio companies can work together to maximize the value of private equity and venture capital investments. This collaborative approach can lead to stronger, more sustainable growth for the portfolio company, while also generating attractive returns for the investor. As the world of private equity and venture capital continues to evolve, it is essential for both investors and portfolio companies to adapt to new challenges and opportunities and to continuously refine their strategies for success.

Chapter 10: Portfolio Management and Value Creation

10.1. Operational Improvements and Growth Strategies

In the realm of private equity and venture capital investments, operational improvements and growth strategies are crucial for maximizing the value of the portfolio companies. Investors often play an essential role in providing strategic guidance, industry expertise, and resources to support and accelerate the growth of their portfolio companies. This chapter delves into various operational improvements and growth strategies that investors and portfolio companies can explore together to create sustainable value.

1. Operational Efficiency: The first step in unlocking value within a portfolio company is often to identify and implement operational efficiencies. This can involve streamlining processes, optimizing supply chain management, and reducing overhead costs. By enhancing operational efficiency, the company can improve its margins, increase profitability, and generate higher returns for investors.

1. Business Process Reengineering: Business process reengineering involves a fundamental rethinking and redesign of core business processes to achieve significant improvements in performance. This can include eliminating redundancies, automating tasks, and reorganizing the company structure to align with strategic objectives. By undergoing business process reengineering, a portfolio company can gain a competitive advantage and drive

sustainable growth.

1. Talent Management: Attracting, retaining, and developing top talent is a critical component of long-term growth and success for any company. Investors can assist portfolio companies in implementing talent management strategies, such as recruitment, employee engagement, professional development, and succession planning. By nurturing a skilled and motivated workforce, the portfolio company can foster innovation and enhance its overall performance.

1. Sales and Marketing Expansion: Another growth strategy is to expand the company's sales and marketing efforts. This may involve entering new markets, launching new products or services, or adopting innovative sales and marketing techniques. Investors can provide industry insights and connections to help the portfolio company identify and capitalize on new opportunities and drive revenue growth.

1. Technology Adoption: Embracing technological advancements can lead to improved efficiency, increased competitiveness, and innovative product offerings. Investors can support the portfolio company in adopting cutting-edge technologies, such as artificial intelligence, machine learning, big data analytics, or blockchain, to revolutionize their operations and create new sources of value.

1. Mergers and Acquisitions: Mergers and acquisitions (M&A) can be an effective strategy for accelerating growth, expanding market share, or diversifying the company's product or service offerings. Investors can provide guidance and resources to help the portfolio company identify, evaluate, and execute strategic M&A transactions that align

with its growth objectives.

1. Financial Restructuring: In some cases, a portfolio company may benefit from financial restructuring to optimize its capital structure, reduce debt, or secure additional financing for growth initiatives. Investors can provide valuable advice and support in navigating the complexities of financial restructuring, ensuring that the portfolio company is well-positioned for future growth.

1. Corporate Governance: Implementing robust corporate governance practices can enhance the portfolio company's transparency, accountability, and risk management. Investors can assist in establishing effective governance structures and processes, including board composition, executive compensation, and internal controls, to support the company's long-term success.

1. Exit Strategy Planning: While growth strategies are vital, it is equally essential for investors and portfolio companies to develop a clear exit strategy. This may involve preparing the company for an initial public offering (IPO), a sale to a strategic buyer, or a secondary buyout. By planning for an eventual exit, the investor can ensure that the portfolio company is well-positioned to maximize value and generate attractive returns.

By pursuing these operational improvements and growth strategies, investors and portfolio companies can work together to create lasting value and drive sustainable success. This collaborative approach can lead to stronger, more resilient businesses that are better positioned to navigate the challenges and opportunities of the ever-evolving private equity and venture capital landscape.

10.2. Monitoring and Risk Management

Investors in private equity and venture capital deals are responsible for monitoring the performance and managing the risks associated with their investments. This is crucial to ensure the success and long-term growth of the portfolio companies, as well as the generation of attractive returns for the investors. This chapter explores the various aspects of monitoring and risk management that investors should consider in their investment strategy.

1. Financial Performance Monitoring: One of the critical aspects of monitoring is regularly assessing the financial performance of the portfolio companies. This involves tracking key financial metrics, such as revenue, EBITDA, net income, and cash flow, as well as evaluating the company's financial statements. By closely monitoring financial performance, investors can identify trends, potential issues, and areas of improvement, enabling them to provide timely guidance and support to the portfolio companies.

1. Operational Performance Monitoring: In addition to financial performance, investors should also monitor the operational performance of their portfolio companies. This can include assessing factors such as production efficiency, customer satisfaction, employee engagement, and market share. By keeping a close eye on operational performance, investors can gain a comprehensive understanding of the company's strengths and weaknesses and identify opportunities for growth and improvement.

1. Governance and Compliance Monitoring: Ensuring that portfolio companies adhere to sound governance practices and comply with relevant laws and regulations is an essential

aspect of monitoring. Investors should review the company's corporate governance structures, policies, and procedures to ensure that they are robust and effective. Additionally, investors should monitor the company's compliance with applicable regulatory requirements, such as securities laws, anti-corruption laws, and environmental regulations, to mitigate legal and reputational risks.

1. Risk Identification and Assessment: As part of the monitoring process, investors should regularly identify and assess the risks associated with their investments. This may involve conducting a thorough risk assessment that considers various risk factors, such as market risks, credit risks, operational risks, legal and regulatory risks, and reputational risks. By identifying and understanding the risks facing their portfolio companies, investors can develop appropriate risk mitigation strategies.

1. Risk Mitigation and Management: Once risks have been identified and assessed, investors should work with their portfolio companies to implement risk mitigation and management strategies. This may involve implementing robust internal controls, improving governance practices, enhancing operational processes, or seeking insurance coverage for certain risks. By actively managing risks, investors can help ensure the long-term success and resilience of their portfolio companies.

1. Portfolio Diversification: One way to manage risk at the portfolio level is through diversification. By investing in a diverse range of companies across different industries, geographies, and stages of development, investors can reduce the impact of any single investment's underperformance on

the overall portfolio. Diversification can help to mitigate risks and enhance the potential for attractive returns across the portfolio.

1. Performance Reporting and Communication: Regular communication and reporting between investors and portfolio companies are vital for effective monitoring and risk management. Investors should establish clear reporting guidelines and expectations, including the frequency and format of performance updates and financial statements. By fostering open and transparent communication, investors can maintain a strong working relationship with their portfolio companies and address any issues or concerns promptly.

1. Ongoing Due Diligence: Although due diligence is often associated with the initial investment decision, ongoing due diligence is a crucial component of monitoring and risk management. Investors should continuously review and update their understanding of the portfolio companies' operations, market dynamics, competitive landscape, and regulatory environment. This ongoing due diligence can help investors anticipate and respond to emerging risks and opportunities effectively.

10.3. Environmental, Social, and Governance (ESG) Considerations

In recent years, Environmental, Social, and Governance (ESG) considerations have become increasingly important for investors, including those in the private equity and venture capital sectors. ESG factors can have a significant impact on the long-term performance and value of a company, and integrating ESG considerations into investment decision-making and portfolio management can lead to more sustainable and resilient investments. This chapter explores the various aspects of ESG considerations that investors should take into account.

1. Understanding ESG Factors: ESG factors encompass a wide range of non-financial issues that can influence a company's performance and value. Environmental factors include climate change, natural resource management, pollution, and waste management. Social factors encompass human rights, labor practices, diversity and inclusion, and community relations. Governance factors relate to corporate governance, board composition, executive compensation, and shareholder rights. Investors should develop a comprehensive understanding of these factors and their potential impact on their portfolio companies.

1. ESG Integration in Investment Decision-Making: Integrating ESG considerations into investment decision-making involves assessing the potential risks and opportunities associated with ESG factors and incorporating this information into the investment analysis and selection process. This may involve evaluating a company's ESG performance, policies, and practices, and considering how these factors may affect the company's financial performance, risk profile, and long-term value creation potential.

1. ESG Due Diligence: As part of the investment process, investors should conduct ESG due diligence on potential portfolio companies. This involves assessing the company's ESG performance, policies, and practices, as well as identifying any potential ESG-related risks or opportunities.

ESG due diligence can help investors identify companies with strong ESG performance, which may be better positioned to manage risks and capitalize on opportunities, leading to more sustainable and resilient investments.

1. ESG Monitoring and Engagement: Once an investment has been made, investors should actively monitor and engage with their portfolio companies on ESG issues. This can involve regularly reviewing the company's ESG performance, policies, and practices, and providing guidance and support on ESG-related matters. Investors can also engage with portfolio companies through various channels, such as board representation, shareholder resolutions, and collaborative initiatives, to promote improved ESG performance and drive positive change.

1. ESG Reporting and Disclosure: Investors should encourage their portfolio companies to adopt robust ESG reporting and disclosure practices. This can help to promote transparency and accountability on ESG matters and provide investors with the information they need to assess the company's ESG performance effectively. Companies that adopt comprehensive ESG reporting, and disclosure practices may also be better positioned to attract capital from a growing pool of ESG-focused investors.

1. ESG Risk Management: Incorporating ESG considerations into risk management processes can help investors identify and manage ESG-related risks more effectively. This may involve integrating ESG factors into the company's risk assessment and mitigation processes, and developing strategies to address ESG-related risks, such as climate change, human rights abuses, and corporate governance

issues.

1. ESG Performance Measurement and Benchmarking: Investors should establish clear ESG performance metrics and benchmarks to assess the ESG performance of their portfolio companies and track progress over time. This can involve adopting standardized ESG reporting frameworks, such as the Global Reporting Initiative (GRI) or the Sustainability Accounting Standards Board (SASB) and comparing the company's ESG performance against industry peers and best practices.

a. By incorporating ESG considerations into their investment strategies and portfolio management practices, investors can not only enhance the sustainability and resilience of their investments but also generate long-term value for their stakeholders. As ESG considerations continue to gain prominence in the investment landscape, private equity and venture capital investors should remain vigilant and proactive in addressing these critical issues.

1. ESG Training and Capacity Building: Investors should provide appropriate training and capacity building for their investment teams and portfolio companies to ensure that they are well-equipped to understand and manage ESG-related risks and opportunities effectively. This may involve offering internal workshops, partnering with external ESG experts, or providing access to resources and tools that can help build knowledge and expertise in ESG matters.

1. Collaboration and Industry Initiatives: Investors can benefit from participating in industry initiatives and collaborating with peers to address ESG challenges and share best practices.

Joining networks and associations, such as the United Nations-supported Principles for Responsible Investment (PRI) or the Global Impact Investing Network (GIIN), can provide access to valuable resources, tools, and insights that can help investors enhance their ESG performance and drive positive change across the industry.

1. ESG and Impact Investing: For some investors, ESG considerations may extend beyond risk management and value creation to encompass a more intentional focus on generating positive social and environmental impact alongside financial returns. Impact investing involves selecting investments that have the potential to deliver measurable, positive impact on specific ESG issues, such as climate change, poverty alleviation, or gender equality. Investors pursuing an impact investing strategy may need to adopt additional tools and methodologies to assess, monitor, and report on the social and environmental impact of their investments, such as the Impact Management Project (IMP) framework or the Global Impact Investing Rating System (GIIRS).

ESG considerations have become an integral part of the investment landscape, and private equity and venture capital investors must remain proactive in addressing these critical issues. By integrating ESG considerations into their investment strategies, due diligence processes, and portfolio management practices, investors can enhance the sustainability and resilience of their investments, drive long-term value creation, and contribute to a more sustainable and equitable future. As the focus on ESG continues to grow, investors who are well-prepared to navigate these complexities will be better positioned to succeed in an increasingly competitive and dynamic market environment.

Part V: Exits and Liquidity Events

Chapter 11: Exit Strategies and Liquidity Events

11.1. Initial Public Offerings (IPOs)

The Initial Public Offering, or IPO, is one of the most high-profile exit strategies for private equity and venture capital investments. An IPO is the process of offering the shares of a private corporation to the public in a new stock issuance. This event provides an opportunity for the company to raise significant capital and for early investors to realize their investment.

The decision to go public is a significant one and is typically driven by a combination of factors. These may include the need for additional capital to fund growth, the desire for liquidity, or the belief that the public market will provide a higher valuation than a private sale or merger.

Before pursuing an IPO, the company and its investors must consider the readiness of the company for the public markets. The company should have a strong and experienced management team, a compelling growth story, a stable and predictable financial performance, and robust internal controls and corporate governance structures. It should also be prepared for the increased scrutiny, disclosure requirements, and regulatory oversight that come with being a public company.

The IPO process is complex and time-consuming, typically taking six to nine months to complete. It involves selecting an underwriting team, preparing the registration statement, conducting the IPO roadshow, and ultimately pricing and selling the shares to the public. The company and its investors will need to work closely with their legal and financial advisors to navigate this process and ensure a successful outcome.

11.2 Mergers and Acquisitions

Another common exit strategy for private equity and venture capital investments is through a merger or acquisition (M&A). This involves the sale of the company to another corporation, which may be a strategic buyer in the same industry or a financial buyer such as a private equity firm.

M&A transactions can provide a quicker and more certain exit than an IPO, as they do not depend on market conditions at a specific point in time. They also avoid the costs, complexities, and regulatory requirements associated with going public. However, they also involve significant negotiation and due diligence, and the final price may be subject to adjustments based on the financial performance of the company or other factors.

The M&A process typically begins with the identification of potential buyers and the preparation of a confidential information memorandum (CIM) that provides detailed information about the company and its financial performance. The company and its advisors will then solicit offers from potential buyers, negotiate the terms of the deal, and conduct due diligence. Once the due diligence is completed and the final terms are agreed, the transaction is formalized in a definitive agreement and closed.

Whether through an IPO or a merger or acquisition, a successful exit requires careful planning, preparation, and execution. Investors should work closely with their portfolio companies and their legal and financial advisors to evaluate the various exit options, prepare for the exit process, and ensure that the company is well-positioned to achieve a successful outcome.

11.3 Secondary Sales and Buyouts

Secondary sales and buyouts are another avenue for exit and liquidity events. A secondary sale typically involves the sale of an investor's stake in a company to another private equity or venture capital firm, or to another type of institutional investor. Secondary sales can offer a path to liquidity when other exit options, such as an IPO or a merger or acquisition, may not be feasible or desirable.

Secondary sales can occur for a variety of reasons. An investor may seek a secondary sale if it needs to generate liquidity, if it is approaching the end of its fund's life, or if it believes that another investor may be better able to support the company's next stage of growth. From the company's perspective, a secondary sale can bring in new investors with additional capital, expertise, and networks to support the company's growth.

Secondary buyouts, a specific type of secondary sale, occur when a private equity firm sells a portfolio company to another private equity firm. These transactions have become increasingly common as the private equity industry has matured and as firms have sought new ways to realize their investments.

11.4 Recapitalizations and Refinancings

Recapitalizations and refinancings are yet another exit strategy, albeit less traditional. In a recapitalization, a company changes its financial structure, typically by issuing new debt to fund a payout to the existing investors. This can provide a partial exit for the investors while allowing them to maintain a stake in the company and participate in its future growth.

Recapitalizations can be an attractive option in certain circumstances. For example, they may be used when the company is generating strong and stable cash flows that can support the additional debt, when the credit markets are favorable, or when the investors believe that the company's value will continue to increase.

However, recapitalizations also carry risks, as they increase the company's leverage and can limit its financial flexibility. Investors and companies considering a recapitalization should carefully evaluate these risks and work with their advisors to structure the transaction appropriately.

11.5 Wind-Downs and Liquidations

In some cases, an exit may involve winding down the company or selling its assets in a liquidation. This is typically the last resort when the company is not performing well and other exit options are not viable. While wind-downs and liquidations do not usually result in a high return for the investors, they can provide some recovery of capital and can be the best option in a difficult situation.

A wind-down or liquidation process needs to be managed carefully to maximize the recovery for the investors and other stakeholders. This may involve selling the company's assets, collecting its receivables, settling its liabilities, and resolving any legal or regulatory issues. The process can be complex and time-consuming, and it may require the assistance of legal and financial advisors, as well as other professionals such as liquidators or insolvency practitioners.

There are various exit strategies available to private equity and venture capital investors, each with its own opportunities and challenges. Investors need to consider these strategies carefully, in light of the specific circumstances of each portfolio company, and work with their advisors to plan and execute the exit process effectively.

Chapter 12: Regulatory Aspects of Exits

12.1. Securities Law Considerations in Exits

When a private equity or venture capital fund is ready to make an exit from an investment, whether through an initial public offering (IPO), a merger or acquisition, or another form of exit, there are numerous securities law considerations that come into play. These considerations can have significant implications for how the exit is structured and executed.

Public Disclosure and Reporting Obligations

If the exit involves an IPO, the company will become a publicly traded company and will be subject to extensive disclosure and reporting obligations under the securities laws. These obligations include the requirement to file a registration statement with the Securities and Exchange Commission (SEC), which discloses detailed information about the company's business, financial condition, management, and risks, as well as the terms of the offering.

After the IPO, the company will be subject to ongoing reporting obligations, including the requirement to file annual reports (Form 10-K), quarterly reports (Form 10-Q), and current reports (Form 8-K) with the SEC. These reports must disclose a wide range of information, and the company must have systems and controls in place to ensure that the reports are accurate, complete, and timely.

Securities Registration and Exemptions

In a merger or acquisition, the securities laws may require the registration of the securities that are being offered to the shareholders of the target company, unless an exemption from registration is available. The specific requirements depend on the structure of the transaction and the types of securities being offered.

One commonly used exemption is Section 4(a)(2) of the Securities Act of 1933, which provides an exemption for transactions not involving any public offering. Another is Rule 506 of Regulation D, which provides a safe harbor for private offerings to accredited investors and up to 35 non-accredited investors.

If the merger or acquisition involves a tender offer, additional rules and regulations will apply, including the tender offer rules under the Securities Exchange Act of 1934 and the rules under the Williams Act.

Insider Trading and Other Fraud Considerations

Insider trading and other forms of securities fraud are serious violations of the securities laws that can result in criminal and civil penalties. In the context of an exit, the company and its insiders must be careful not to trade on the basis of material nonpublic information or to make false or misleading statements to the market.

State Securities Laws

In addition to federal securities laws, each state has its own securities laws, often referred to as "blue sky" laws. These laws vary from state to state, but they generally require the registration of securities offerings unless an exemption is available. In some cases, the state laws may also impose additional disclosure requirements or other obligations.

In sum, the securities laws have significant implications for exits by private equity and venture capital funds. It is essential for the funds and their legal advisors to understand these implications and to structure and execute the exit in compliance with the applicable laws.

12.2. Tax Implications of Exit Transactions

The tax implications of an exit transaction can significantly influence the net return to investors and the economic outcome of the deal. These implications depend on various factors, including the structure of the transaction, the nature of the assets being sold, the characteristics of the seller and the buyer, and the tax jurisdictions involved.

Structure of the Transaction

Exit transactions can be structured in different ways, each with distinct tax implications. In general, transactions can be structured as asset sales, stock sales, or mergers.

- Asset Sales: In an asset sale, the company sells its assets to the buyer. The proceeds of the sale are first used to pay off the company's liabilities, and the remaining proceeds are distributed to the shareholders. This type of sale may result in double taxation. The company pays tax on the gain from the sale of the assets, and the shareholders pay tax on the distribution of the proceeds. Asset sales can be beneficial, however, when the assets have a low tax basis and the company has net operating losses that can offset the gain.

- Stock Sales: In a stock sale, the shareholders sell their shares to the buyer. The shareholders pay tax on the gain from the sale of the stock, but the company does not pay any tax. This type of sale is generally more tax-efficient than an asset sale, but it may be less attractive to the buyer, who takes on all the liabilities of the company and gets a "step-up" in the basis of the assets.

- Mergers: In a merger, the company is combined with another company. The tax implications of a merger depend on whether it is structured as a taxable or tax-free merger. In a taxable merger, the shareholders pay tax on the gain from the exchange of their shares for the shares or assets of the acquiring company. In a tax-free merger, the exchange of shares is not taxed, but the shareholders take on a carryover basis in the shares of the acquiring company.

Nature of the Assets Being Sold

The nature of the assets being sold can also have significant tax implications. If the assets include capital assets or Section 1231 assets (which include depreciable property and real property used in a trade or business), the gain from the sale of these assets is generally taxed at preferential capital gain rates. However, if the assets include inventory or accounts receivable, the gain from the sale of these assets is taxed as ordinary income.

Characteristics of the Seller and the Buyer

The tax characteristics of the seller and the buyer can also affect the tax implications of an exit transaction. For example, if the seller is a corporation, the transaction may be subject to double taxation, as described above. If the seller is a pass-through entity, such as a partnership or an S corporation, the transaction is generally subject to only one level of tax.

The tax characteristics of the buyer can also affect the structure of the transaction. For example, a buyer that can use net operating losses may prefer an asset sale, which can generate a step-up in the basis of the assets and create new depreciation or amortization deductions.

Tax Jurisdictions Involved

Finally, the tax jurisdictions involved in the transaction can have significant implications. Each jurisdiction may have its own rules regarding the taxation of business transactions. In an international transaction, the tax rules of the jurisdictions where the seller, the buyer, and the company are located can all come into play.

It is essential to involve tax advisors early in the process to understand these implications and structure the transaction in a tax-efficient manner as the tax implications of an exit transaction are complex and can have a significant impact on the economic outcome of the deal.

12.3. Antitrust and Competition Regulations

Antitrust and competition regulations are crucial considerations during exit transactions, particularly for mergers and acquisitions (M&As). These rules are designed to promote competition and prevent market domination, which could be detrimental to consumers. Violating these regulations can lead to significant penalties, including fines and forced dissolution of business combinations. Hence, a thorough understanding of these regulations is essential for private equity and venture capital firms, as well as their portfolio companies, especially during exit transactions.

U.S. Antitrust Law

In the United States, the key antitrust laws include the Sherman Act, the Clayton Act, and the Federal Trade Commission Act. These laws prohibit agreements that restrict competition (such as price-fixing or bid-rigging), monopolization, and certain mergers and acquisitions that may substantially lessen competition.

When evaluating M&As, the Department of Justice (DOJ) and the Federal Trade Commission (FTC) consider factors such as market share, market concentration, barriers to entry, and the potential for anti-competitive effects. If a transaction is found to potentially lessen competition, the agencies can challenge it in court, and if they prevail, the transaction may be blocked or unwound.

Notification and Review Process

Under the Hart-Scott-Rodino (HSR) Act, parties to certain large M&As must notify the FTC and the DOJ of their proposed transaction and observe a waiting period before closing the deal. This allows the agencies to investigate the potential effects on competition and take action if necessary. The HSR thresholds are adjusted annually; as of 2023, the size-of-transaction threshold is $92 million.

Once an HSR notification is filed, a 30-day waiting period begins (15 days for cash tender offers or bankruptcy sales). During this period, the agencies review the submitted materials and may request additional information (known as a "second request"), which extends the waiting period. Parties cannot close their transaction until the waiting period has expired or been terminated.

Global Competition Law Considerations

In an increasingly globalized economy, cross-border M&As may be subject to competition laws of multiple jurisdictions. For example, the European Union enforces competition law across its member states through the European Commission. Its regulations are similar to those in the U.S., prohibiting anti-competitive agreements and abuses of dominant positions, and requiring pre-merger notification for certain transactions.

Other countries, such as Canada, Australia, China, and Brazil, also have their own competition laws and review processes. Therefore, for cross-border transactions, it's essential to consider these international requirements and coordinate filings in various jurisdictions.

Strategies to Address Antitrust Risks

Given the significant implications of antitrust and competition regulations, parties to an M&A transaction should assess potential antitrust risks early in the process. This might involve conducting a preliminary antitrust analysis, considering potential remedies to address competition concerns (such as divestitures), and developing a strategy for regulatory filings.

In some cases, parties may structure a deal in a certain way to minimize antitrust risks. For example, they might choose an asset purchase rather than a merger if the former is less likely to raise competition concerns.

Moreover, the antitrust review process should be factored into the transaction timeline. While most transactions are cleared in the initial HSR waiting period, a second request or a competition investigation in another jurisdiction can significantly extend the process.

Due to the significant impact that antitrust and competition regulations can have on exit transactions, it is highly recommended that parties should consider seeking advice from legal experts specializing in antitrust law in order to navigate these complexities.

Conclusion

Throughout the journey of this book, we have delved into the intricacies of securities law as it applies to the world of private equity and venture capital. From the formation of funds to exit strategies, we have covered a plethora of topics to provide an insider's guide into this dynamic and complex field. The goal was to provide not only a theoretical perspective but also a practical guide for legal practitioners, business professionals, and students alike.

We began our journey with an introduction to the world of private equity and venture capital, understanding the role these players have in shaping industries and innovating economies. We then traversed through the legal intricacies of fund formation, exploring entities, structures, and the pivotal roles of limited and general partners. Tax considerations were another significant aspect we looked into, understanding the implications at both the domestic and international levels.

Regulatory authorities play a crucial role in this field, and we provided a comprehensive overview of key U.S. regulatory bodies, including the SEC, FINRA, CFTC, and state regulators. We delved into the importance of registration, exemptions, and compliance, focusing on fiduciary duties and the management of conflicts of interest. The JOBS Act and its implications for emerging growth companies were also highlighted.

We took a deep dive into Anti-Money Laundering (AML) and Know Your Customer (KYC) compliance, which are paramount in today's global economy. We also explored deal flow and networking, understanding the importance of due diligence, both legal and financial, as well as industry-specific considerations.

When it came to the deal itself, we explored terms, negotiation, financing, and capital structure, followed by a look into the closing and post-closing phases. Post-investment, we examined operational improvements, risk management, and the growing importance of Environmental, Social, and Governance (ESG) considerations.

Exit strategies and liquidity events, including IPOs and M&As, were also discussed in detail, delving into their securities law considerations, tax implications, and antitrust and competition regulations.

As we conclude this comprehensive guide, it is important to remember that the world of private equity and venture capital is highly dynamic and ever evolving. This means that while this book provides a detailed overview and practical guide, staying updated with changes in laws, regulations, and industry practices is essential. It is our hope that this book serves as a strong foundation upon which you can build your understanding and navigate the complex yet exciting world of private equity and venture capital.

Appendix: Glossary of Key Terms

1. Anti-Money Laundering (AML): A set of procedures, laws, and regulations designed to stop the practice of generating income through illegal actions and make it more difficult for those engaged in illegal activities to hide the proceeds of their crimes.

1. Commodity Futures Trading Commission (CFTC): An independent agency of the US government that regulates futures and options markets.

1. Due Diligence: An investigation or audit of a potential investment or product to confirm all facts and assess its potential risks.

1. Emerging Growth Companies: Under the JOBS Act, a company with total annual gross revenues of less than $1.07 billion during its most recently completed fiscal year is considered an emerging growth company.

1. Financial Industry Regulatory Authority (FINRA): A private, self-regulatory organization that polices brokerage firms and exchange markets in the United States.

1. General Partner (GP): A partner who is actively involved in the day-to-day operations of the partnership and has unlimited liability for the debts of the partnership.

1. Initial Public Offering (IPO): The first sale of stock by a company to the public.

1. Know Your Customer (KYC): The process of a business

verifying the identity of its clients and assessing their suitability, along with the potential risks of illegal intentions towards the business relationship.

1. Limited Partner (LP): An investor in a limited partnership who is not involved in the day-to-day operations and has limited liability for the debts of the partnership.

1. Private Equity (PE): Equity capital that is not quoted on a public exchange, used for the acquisition of private companies or the privatization of public companies.

1. Securities and Exchange Commission (SEC): A US government oversight agency responsible for regulating the securities industry.

1. Venture Capital (VC): Financing that investors provide to startup companies and small businesses that are believed to have long-term growth potential.

1. Tax Structuring: The arrangement of a business's operations to minimize tax liabilities.

1. Environmental, Social, and Governance (ESG): A set of standards for a company's operations that socially conscious investors use to screen potential investments.

Index

About the Author

Josh is a data scientist and a prolific author of books on artificial intelligence, geopolitics, finance and cybersecurity. With several books on these subjects under his belt, Josh has established himself as a thought leader in the field. His most recent books, "Silent Wars: Espionage, Sabotage, and the Covert Battles in Cyberspace", "Silicon and Rare Earth: The Global Contest for Semiconductor and Rare Earth Supremacy", AGI Architects: Building a Symbiotic Civilization with Superintelligent Systems", "Algorithmic Warfare: The Rise of Autonomous Weapons", and "The Geopolitics of Artificial Intelligence: Strategic Implications of AI for Global Security" highlight his deep understanding of the historically unprecedented impact that artificial intelligence is poised to have on the future of the human race. His books have been praised for their practical advice and actionable insights, making them must-reads for anyone looking to gain a better understanding of the implications of emerging technologies for our society, our environment, and our future.

In addition to being an author, Josh is the host of Innovate Now: The Pulse of Future Technologies, a podcast that explores the fascinating world of emerging technologies and the future of innovation by delving into the most groundbreaking advancements in artificial intelligence, fintech, distributed and quantum computing, the AI arms race, and the tech start-up ecosystem. Josh is also a seasoned practitioner. He is the founder of a number of startup companies including one that is focused on AI research and another that provides cybersecurity consulting services, and performs penetration testing engagements.

Josh is committed to staying at the forefront of the rapidly evolving field of emerging technologies. His expertise and passion have made him a sought-after speaker and consultant, and his contributions have been widely recognized and appreciated. Whether through his books, his work with clients, or his field assignments, Josh continues to inspire and educate others in the hope of making a lasting impact on the world of artificial intelligence and cybersecurity. If you're looking for practical and actionable insights be sure to check out Josh's other manuscripts and join his community of readers and followers.

www.ingramcontent.com/pod-product-compliance
Lightning Source LLC
LaVergne TN
LVHW090418210926
848480LV00002B/607